IT TAKES ALL 5

Praise for

IT TAKES ALL 5

"Never having been a single mom, at least not in this lifetime, I was quite surprised at how much I enjoyed Kerri's well-written, filled with good sense, and light-hearted rendition of the potential inherent in relationship at any age. As a guy, I found the way she shares with women enabled me to see that I could use her very same guidelines should I find myself on the male end of seeking a meaningful relationship."

H. Ronald Hulnick, Ph.D., President, University of Santa Monica, and co-author with Mary R. Hulnick, Ph.D., *Loyalty To Your Soul: The Heart of Spiritual Psychology*

"Filled with wise perspectives, solid information and insightful personal stories, '*It Takes all 5*' is a smart guide for single moms who want to take control of their lives, inside and out, for a more enriching happily ever after."

Michael Levine, Best-selling author and prominent media expert.

"Finally! A book for single mothers about dating that goes beyond the typical 'what to wear' and 'where to meet men' approach. In, '*It Takes All 5: A Single Mom's Guide To Finding The REAL One*' Kerri Zane not only gives the single mother 'permission' to date, she also manages the near-impossible by taking a much-discussed subject and adding elements that to this point, are rarely if ever addressed. Kerri combines compelling the reader to examine, discover and reinvent herself from the inside-out with practical elements, such as physical and financial well-being. This book promises to be a welcome, breath-of-fresh-air addition to any single mother's library."

Carole Brody Fleet, Award-winning and bestselling author, *"Widows Wear Stilettos..."* and *"Happily EVEN After..."*

"Most of us look at the 'celebrity type' lifestyle as one to be envied and perfect. Kerri Zane's personal experience allows all of us to look at our lives, appreciate the strength within and not to 'judge a book by its cover.' How refreshing to read raw honesty. Kerri makes it simple- we are all going through the same struggles! As a single Mom, I am not unique in what I have experienced but the wisdom I share has allowed me the honor of meeting a beautifully courageous woman like Kerri. Thank you Kerri for sharing your life with all of us and giving us the strength and courage to just keep going! You don't have to be a super hero; you just have to never give up no matter what the challenge is."

Helen Georgaklis Founder, CEO of the best selling series, *99 Book Series* (www.99-series.com) and the *Kids Write Club* (www.kidswriteclub.com)

"'It Takes All 5'... is an exceptional insight into the psyche of transcending through the many stages of finding one's self, and the real true love of your life. Being a film and television Producer, A New York Times Best Selling Author, a Journalist, and most of all a One Time Single Father of Three, I feel Kerri Zane's book applies to females and males alike. I wish I had it during my growth years. It would have made the transition a more pleasurable one."

Larry Garrison "The NewsBreaker" and President of SilverCreek Entertainment

"Combining compelling interviews from real single moms, substantive research and the "no fail" five-finger Philosophy for finding true love, Zane has written a sassy, breezy and soulful must read for single moms everywhere."

Mark Freeman Executive Producer –
Original Programming Veria Living Network

"Read this book, and prepare to know that only through being tested in life, can you really achieve the happiness and wisdom we all seek. Know that Kerri has been on a journey of self-exploration her entire life, and now strives to share her real world experiences (the good and the bad) to help others find their personal road to happiness as well."

Lee Gaither, Television Executive/Producer, MGM Studios

"Kerri Zane's book – '*It Takes All 5...*' — illuminates an overlooked aspect of profound and increasing importance in modern life. Her writing about single mothers presents interesting new information, factually accurate in content along with helpful life insights to achieve more wonderful life and living. This book is a must read for single mothers and for others concerned, connected, or wishing to connect with a single mother."

Dr. Gordon Patzer, Author of,
"*Looks: Why They Matter More Than You Ever Imagined*"
director and founder of the, "Appearance Research Institute"

"Kerri Zane is one of the finest female Lifestyle Television executives in the business. She has her fingers on the pulse of what is important to women and knows how to bring stories to life in a compelling and innovative manner."

Mark Teitelbaum, Personal Manager,
Producer/Owner — Teitelbaum & Associates

"Kerri is one of the brightest and most energetic talents I've had the pleasure of working with in recent years. Her passion for helping single mom's overcome life's obstacles is unmatched. She is recommended reading for all women."

Bob Brill, News Anchor/Author/Screenwriter, KNX News Radio (CA) *"Fan Letters to a Stripper: A Patti Waggin Tale"* and *"NO BARRIER: How the Internet Destroyed the World Economy."*

"A must read for any single mom looking for a better and brighter happily ever after."

Melissa G. Wilson, Author, *"Networlding"* and *"Networking is Dead."*

"Having spent many years working with women who struggle to find the balance between kids, working and romance, Kerri Zane's new book *"It Takes All 5,"* is the perfect guide for a healthy and happy life after divorce."

Jay Firestone, founder and president of Prodigy Pictures

IT TAKES ALL 5

*A Single
Mom's Guide
to Finding
the REAL One*

KERRI ZANE

New York

IT TAKES ALL 5
A Single Mom's Guide to Finding the REAL One

ISBN 978-1-61448-186-7 paperback
ISBN 978-1-61448-187-4 eBook
Library of Congress Control Number: 2011944807

Morgan James Publishing
The Entrepreneurial Publisher
5 Penn Plaza, 23rd Floor,
New York City, New York 10001
(212) 655-5470 office • (516) 908-4496 fax
www.MorganJamesPublishing.com

Cover Design by:
Rachel Lopez
www.r2cdesign.com

Interior Design by:
Bonnie Bushman
bonnie@caboodlegraphics.com

In an effort to support local communities, raise awareness and funds, Morgan James Publishing donates a percentage of all book sales for the life of each book to Habitat for Humanity Peninsula and Greater Williamsburg.

Get involved today, visit
www.MorganJamesBuilds.com.

This book is dedicated to the loving memory of my dad
Ervin Samuel Zane
His strength and fearlessness always showed me the way,
And his unflinching support was a constant comfort
August 1926 —April 2007

Table of Contents

Preface

Successful people do what unsuccessful people don't dare.
—Anonymous

Just Like Everyone Else

Though it appeared to the outside world that my marriage was fairy-tale perfect, it was, in truth, no Cinderella story. By the time my husband and I separated, I was 43 years old and already had one divorce under my belt stemming from a brief but challenging relationship in my early 20s. So after 12 additional years of matrimony (this time with two young children's lives to take into consideration), it wasn't as easy to walk away.

Contrary to what those closest to me thought, I didn't wake up one morning from a premenopausal night sweat and capriciously decide it was time to shake things up and get another divorce. Despite all of the fine requisite trappings the nuptials begat, including the "rock" (my big diamond ring, beautiful home, fancy vacations and fast cars) and "paper" (my hand-painted marriage contract), somewhere along the line, the "scissors" cut something out. I think it was the heart.

After a lot of trepidation and several years of therapy, I made the truly painful choice to move on with my life. I believed that there could be a different kind of relationship for me, one that would bring a deeper and more meaningful love.

Following an appropriate reprieve for marital mourning, I hit the singles scene with the intention of giving myself the best shot at finding forever-after true love. But the dynamics of dating and mating were radically different from my first go-round. As an older, more mature single woman, I discovered that I was seen as less desirable than the nubile princess that I was in my youth. At 43 years of age, many men considered me three years past my "best used by" date. I came saddled with the accountability for two young children as well as my aging mom. This frequently made me unavailable when the whim struck to simply hook up.

I found that seeing my belly crinkle from that dang stretched-out baby-birthing skin that won't go away is not sexy. I had a nasty set of unrelenting, Botox-impregnable wrinkles lining my brow and an unwieldy load of financial responsibilities. If all that wasn't enough to make me undateable, I was engulfed in divorce proceedings that shook me to my emotional core. With my litany of woes, it didn't seem as if I, or any one of my other single-mom sisters with whom I coffee-klatched, would be able to master the art of snagging an authentic, romantic real love.

Standing in the face of my misgivings, I staunchly refused to give up my belief that we were all entitled to that opportunity.

The Outside 5

I figured all I needed to do was resculpt myself into great shape! My abs went from post-baby flab to hot-mama fab. I received my ACE personal training certification and learned all the latest in nutrition for a healthy weight-management program. I got plenty of male attention for my outside, but the relationships with these guys (and I am using the word *relationship* loosely) weren't sustainable. Each time a liaison failed (my track record over a nine-year period was three months max—maybe six if we didn't spend a bunch of time together), I'd be devastated and confused.

Don't get me wrong—exercise and healthy nutrition are important and actually critical to your overall well-being. I truly believe that I could not have either accomplished what I did or overcome all the challenges from my divorce had I not gained the confidence accomplished through my training. However, fitness couldn't bring me the unfaltering commitment from real love that I so desired because it couldn't take away the pain and internal scarring I'd suffered from the past. I wasn't healthy on the inside. I never stopped to take stock of all the events that had led me to that place. The stories that I'd constructed in my head about myself from early childhood would play out over and over again, perpetuating the negative patterns I'd come to know as "my life." I created this fearful place that was bereft of all self-worth, self-love, and self-acceptance.

The Inside 5

It was time to heal the whole woman inside, along with the outside. Through my University of Santa Monica Master's Program in Spiritual Psychology and extensive related research, I learned important life and empowerment skills that gave me a spiritual grounding with a broad emotional baseline to add to my already mental approach. I began to embrace compassionate self-forgiveness, worked on rescripting my story, truly listened to my intuition, and understood my ability to make choices.

My two beautiful daughters allowed me 10 years of trial-and-error in-the-trenches training as a single parent, and I became the best mom I could be. Helping my own mother mourn the loss of her husband and heal after a near deadly bout of shingles taught me the importance of drawing from a deep inner pool of compassion. I spent many hours and gained enormous wisdom interviewing hundreds of other single mothers between the ages of 25 and 85. I started having healthier relationships with everyone in my life, including myself.

The "REAL ONE" 5

I shifted my beliefs about the constructs of what true love really means. I began to reconsider my own dating experiences as enjoyable and educational opportunities rather than prospecting ventures for finding a new husband. I rescripted every encounter as a way to learn more about who I was and what qualities I wanted in a complete physical, mental, emotional, spiritual, and sexual long-term relationship.

This 10-year journey has led me to develop a healthy new way of being and the most effective method to finding not just the "the One" but "the REAL One" for an authentic and renewable "REAL"ationship. I call it the 5 Finger Philosophy. What I've outlined in this book is a powerful, life altering, and empowering guide for all single moms to ultimately and once and for all have their true love. Which, I am happy to tell you, I have found—and so can everyone!

Acknowledgments

It Takes All 5 is the result of my own 10 year personal journey of growth and discovery. Every step of the way has been a result of the extraordinary people in my life who have supported, inspired, and encouraged me as well as of the amazing women who shared their love, light, and wisdom. They are the heart and soul of this book and living examples that there is, in fact, a beautiful life ever after.

First and foremost, to my daughters, Rachele and Daniele Friedland, you are the two brightest shining lights in my life. You are both so wise beyond your years and are such loving and caring young women. You make me proud to be your mom. What we share in our warm, peaceful, crazy, wacky, funny, inviting "sorority-like" love- (and kitty-) filled home makes life a really cool place to be! You are my daily inspiration. Thank you.

To my mom, Anne Zane, who loves me so much and always shares her pearls of wisdom as she sees the world through her 92-year-young eyes. You are my rock and constant inspiration. You prove to me every day that women are amazingly resilient and strong. The body may break, but the brain stays sharp, and one can always find light in humor even in the darkest and most painful of days. Thank you for caring about my happiness and supporting me as I follow my dreams.

To my beautiful Latin sister, Gloria Rodriguez: You are my beacon. I could not survive a day without you. Your unfailing love, guidance, wisdom, and support have been the biggest gifts in my life.

To my big sister, Carol Pedersen: Without you, my day-to-day existence would not be possible. Your wisdom, strength, guidance, and support have afforded me the opportunity to be the self-reliant single mom I wanted to be.

To all my darling friends and family—especially Syndee Schwartz, Mindy Casas, Sue Steinberg, Marni Bernstein, Larry Garrison, Greg Bingham, Jay Firestone, Mark Freeman and Peter Greenberg—thank you for your love and support through this writing process and eagerly encouraged me to keep going.

I want to thank each and every woman who granted me an interview and so openly shared her stories of strength, fortitude, and self-reliance. You are all the true heart and soul of this book.

My utmost gratitude to my teachers and light workers, Ron and Mary Hulnick; the University of Santa Monica community, especially my project team, Kyle Brace and Juliana Guerriero; and the educators at Landmark Education who helped me heal my wounds, change my perspectives, see my rescripted path with grace and ease, and allow me a space to create a beautiful new living vision for the rest of my life.

I would like to thank Michael Ebeling, who led me to my publishers, Morgan James. Gratitude also goes to all the beautiful souls at Morgan James Publishers—Lyza Poulin, David Hancock, Jim Howard, Bethany Marshall, and Rick Frishman—who made the publishing process seem effortless and easy.

A special thank you to Carole Brody Fleet, who inspired me to get going on this silly dream I had of writing a book in the first place.

Most of all, I thank Michael Rosenthal. Without you, this book would NEVER have been the body of work that it is. You are not only my REAL One but also my beautiful soul partner and best friend. I am so appreciative of all your thoughts, ideas, inspirations, contributions, time, and patience reading and rereading. This book and the vision I set out to make a reality could not have been possible without your love and support. The gratitude I feel for having you in my life is inexpressible.

Introduction

*The hunger for love is much more difficult to
remove than the hunger for bread.*
—Mother Teresa

No matter how young or old, there is a true love out there for every woman who seeks it. Many call this person "The One." But for single moms, that "One" might not have worked out so well. Perhaps you married your high school sweetheart and were just too young to know better, or you waited so long that you worried it would never happen, so you settled for the only one who asked. Or, tragically, you've lost your true love and are now widowed.

Finding yourself suddenly living solo in a "plus-one world" can be disconcerting. In spite of the fact that there are millions of single mothers out there, each of us still feels as though we are traversing unchartered territory. We awkwardly stand unaccompanied at cocktail parties, weddings, and holiday events. We mingle alone at Back-to-School nights among the other coupled parents and feel out of place. We go to children's birthday parties where the moms and dads of other young ones are planning family retreats together—the "unpaired" don't get invited. We stand in the schoolyard with the other married moms waiting for our kids to jet forth when the school bell rings while the married mothers whisper in hushed tones, secretly threatened that we're conspiring to steal their precious husbands. My name for this "affliction": "The Scarlet Letter Syndrome."

We single moms silently struggle with myriad tough questions swirling in our heads. How do we balance having a full life for ourselves while being a top-notch parent to our children? Do we want to enter a relationship again? Will we even get a second chance? Will there be a man out there who will accept our children and us? More importantly, will he be respectful of our role as mother, and will he be good to our children? Is there such a thing as a soul mate? What does it take to make a better choice this time around? What is the meaning of a truly authentic loving relationship? If we find it, will we recognize it and know how to keep it? And the most troubling question of all: Do we uphold societal expectations and eventually trust marriage again, or is there a different way for us to create a lasting loving relationship?

Can we find The REAL One? Is it possible to have a REALationship?

The truth is that transition is difficult no matter what or who caused the life shift. There is important all-encompassing work to be done inside and outside to make ourselves healthy before taking the leap into the next romantic liaison. It is virtually impossible for anyone to enter into a fulfilling new relationship in a balanced way without the kind of support that this book provides.

"It Takes All 5…" is divided into three distinct sections.

Part One, titled "The Inside 5," aptly focuses on healing the "inside woman."

It is the ability to have clarity about who you are on the inside to create the foundation for making the life-altering transformations on the outside. In Chapter 1, you will discover that there are three pivotal stories that need rescripting. When the stories are identified and repurposed with revised choices, the wheels will be set in motion to open up a place in your heart for The REAL One to show up.

You have half a glass of champagne sitting in front of you. Do you see it as practically empty, or nearly brimming over? The way you perceive every aspect of what goes on in your world has an impact on how you live your daily life. No matter what gauntlet gets tossed in your path, only you have the power to rescript it. It can be a pitch-black nightmare or a golden opportunity. Chapter 2 outlines a decidedly upbeat approach that will help you distinguish the silver lining in all of your possibilities.

Chapter 3 is a virtual tour through the darker side of your psyche. It is here that we sweep clean the cobwebs of that nasty four-letter feeling which causes the glass-half-empty point of view: fear. You will find that the best way to erase the most heinous of happiness hiccups, oddly enough, is to embrace them. There are some key strategies to undertake that will help you face every one of your fears head-on. Ultimately, they will dissipate and eventually lose their hold on you.

Chapter 4 will help you key in on identifying when you are truly getting what you want and need out of life instead of continuing to play the quintessential fem people-pleaser role that has you appeasing everyone else in your universe. There is an important distinction made in understanding the difference between your truth and the truth. You will find that having the gumption to trust your intuition is vastly fulfilling. It will also help you authentically portray the real you to your REAL One.

Chapter 5 is a road map to the here and now. As unsettling as it might seem, we can only live in this very moment—there are no others. The past has already happened, and there is nothing we can do to change what's already occurred. The future is a provocative and beguiling space that we can hope for, but we're still uncertain about the eventual outcome. It is surprising what often shows up when you learn to appreciate the absolute joy in the here-and-now.

Part Two, titled "The Outside 5," aptly focuses on healing the "outside woman."

In Chapter 6 you will take a southbound turn back to age two, when saying no was a simple two-letter word. In those days, you used it with reckless abandon. Now you need to be a bit more judicious, tenderly placing it in the right spots. The ability to blurt "NO!" when it serves you best will make your life a much nicer place to reside.

Chapter 7 deals with the delicate issues of divorce dollars and cents. How you choose to end your marriage can set the tone for your continuing relationship with your children's dad. You have choices. There are also many financial options to consider that are absolutely vital to handle logically and with prudence for the welfare of you and your children.

Chapters 8 and 9 are near and dear to my heart, as they speak to the soul of your outer core. The body is our vessel. For single moms in search of finding The REAL One, this is especially true. It not only stores your heart, but it is also your calling card. By loving yourself first and taking care of your exterior details, it allows you to stay in the game and banish the confidence crashers that line your skin and belie your age. Here is where you will come face-to-face with all that is keeping you from putting your best face forward. These chapters contain all the how and whys for the best beauty and body meld to make you the complete package for your true love. Chapter 10 focuses on the how, where, when and why it's never too late to get your sexy back.

Part three, titled "The REAL One 5," takes you to the heart of this book. It is where everything comes together for finding The REAL One and creating a REALationship.

After having done all the inside and outside work, you are ready to emerge and spread your wings, just like the butterfly who has been cocooned. Chapters 11 through 13 will take a look at where to go, what to do and how to be in order to attain your perfect REAL One. Why *the REAL One?* Because when you join together with this man, he will be not just the one, but also the REAL deal! It will be your best, true love REALationship. To have a REALationship that is sustainable for the long-term requires having the REAL One.

Chapter 14 outlines how to find the REAL One to create a REALationship using the Five-Finger Philosophy. Chapter 15 explains the various options to consider when, once he's found, how to keep your REAL One—for as long as you both choose.

And for additional information or to learn more about putting the topics in this book to work in your life, visit www.kerrizane.com.

Part One:

THE INSIDE 5

1 RESCRIPT YOUR LIFE

Your story is not what happens to you in life; rather it
is what you make happen in your life that is your story.
—Kerri Zane

Humans are meant to exist in pairs, and I am sure you thought when you married "Him" that you were done with that "searching for your perfect match" business. Now as a single mom, when you reflect on your life, you are a little bit older; yes, definitely wiser; for sure, perhaps carrying a few extra pounds; and no doubt ruled by your children's agenda. The prospect of starting over again to find another significant other can feel overwhelming and the task of connecting with a new mate hopeless.

But let's face it. You need time to take a deep breath and turn what most might consider a sad loss into a golden opportunity. Assess everything about you and rediscover who you really are now as a uniquely special single mom. Then give yourself the space to uncover who will fulfill you best as you move forward for the rest of your life. What you discover will allow you to make any and all the changes you see fit in order to be the best you can be. Then it will be easy to follow your heart and find the REAL One.

Grieve And Go On

Grief is primarily the pain of resisting what is.
— John Welshons

Before you take one step forward, allow yourself the privilege and time to mourn the past. Grieving is perfectly understandable when you've lost your significant other to illness or accident, but many do not allow themselves to do so with divorce. It is a loss. Regardless of the circumstances, it triggers the same emotions. You become suddenly unsure of who you are and how you should be when not defined by a marriage. Everything about your life changes—the street route you take to drop your kids off at school, responsibilities around your house, finances, and your relationships with every friend and family member in your circle.

Change is stressful, and a lot of changes at once are even more challenging. Divorce is number two on the list of most stressful events. So naturally, the healing will take time. Give yourself permission to have different feelings and the time to function at less than 100 percent. It's perfectly normal to have lots of ups and downs and feel many conflicting emotions, including anger, resentment, sadness, relief, fear, betrayal, and confusion. It's important to identify and acknowledge these feelings. While these emotions will often be painful, trying to suppress or ignore them will only prolong the grieving process. Share your feelings with friends and family so they can help you get through this period. Not only do you need their emotional support but you also need people to help fill the social calendar that was more than likely previously filled by your former spouse. If necessary, don't be afraid to get outside professional help. Isolating yourself can raise your stress levels, reduce your concentration, and get in the way of your work, relationships, and overall health. Most importantly, accept that all these reactions are normal and will lessen over time. In *The Power of Full Engagement*, authors Jim Loehr and Tony Schwartz give counsel that grief, like most toxic emotions, is best metabolized in waves, intermittently opening up the energy channel to allow the sadness in and then seeking recovery in the form of comfort, laughter, hope, and reengagement. You will find that eventually, the mourning will dissipate and be replaced by an overwhelming curiosity to rediscover yourself.

Start With Your Backstory

*Too many people overvalue what they are
not and undervalue what they are.*
—Malcolm S. Forbes

The best way to begin to uncover who you truly are is by starting at the beginning of your story. From birth to this point, you are amalgams of your life experiences. They are the events and interactions with others that have defined you, from childhood games of playing house in cardboard boxes to tumultuous adult bedroom alliances. Each scene of your life blends with the others to create your story—or at least the story about you that you've scripted so far. Your story is, in fact, just a story. The beauty of the life you live is that you can rescript your story any time you want!

You are the scribe of every scene in your life. So, you are the one who gets to choose how you want to be in your story, which direction you want the story to take, and how you want to interpret it. In other words, your entire life is based on your scene translations and your personal choices. Unfortunately, you can't see into your own future, so it is not always clear what the consequences of your choices will be or how you will hold those stories in your mind. Like many women, you probably define the results of your choices—the subsequent experiences—as either "good" or "bad." You judge yourself as "wrong" if your choices don't work out the way you intended.

Defining events that occur as good or bad presupposes that you are a casualty rather than a power player in your own life. Admittedly, some of your choices have been or will be better than others, but the beauty of having the ability to choose is that you are in charge of what happens to you. And with every choice you make, for better or worse, there are lessons to be learned and personal growth to be attained. That is really what your life and being in relationship are all about.

The more you learn and grow, the more confident a woman you will become. You'll no longer need to live the "he's just not that into you" reality nor will you ever need to settle for someone less than ideal. What I'm talking about is you being ready when The REAL One enters your orbit. You get to choose *him*!

In order to break your "woe is me" pattern, you will need to reflect on your key life experiences and change your interpretation and choice. These events and your responses (or thoughts, beliefs, and ultimately, choices) to these events have led you to become who you are today. Your thoughts became your beliefs, and your beliefs became your story. Now, it's your choice to redefine the experience and rescript a whole new story to create the enviable new life you desire.

Rescript: Act One

Confidence is feeling satisfied with who and what we are.
—Anonymous

Locked inside every woman's brain are three profound life-defining experiences. The first occurs early in her life, some time between the ages of two and five. First of all, no one, including you, could imagine that a child under five years old could be responsible for any kind of traumatic event such as abandonment, abuse, or social exclusion. Second, you did the best you could to understand the distressing events in light of your age and the circumstances. Science has found strong evidence that young children are incapable of processing any childhood traumas because the cortices in their brains are not fully developed. Without that capacity to make sense of an event, the feeling part of the brain takes over, and you react emotionally from environmental cues. If these emotions are not effectively dealt with, they create lifetime scars. You end up seeing yourself within the context of how the people in your life scripted your story. Further, you are not alone; the majority of all adult women have suffered some type of childhood trauma.

For me, it was the morning my birth father got up out of bed, packed up his golf clubs, and moved out of our house. He left my mom with two young children—my brother and me— and a lot of debt. He never returned to be a part of our lives.

> I grew up knowing I had a birth father that didn't care. His departure left me feeling abandoned and a mess for the majority of my life.

The impact of my birth father not showing up in my life has been a continual open wound that resurfaced over and over again in my romantic relationships. In my childhood story, I believed I was responsible for his departure because I was a bad girl. So growing up, I believed if I were really good no matter what the cost, I would never be the one abandoned again. In adulthood, I became the Queen of the Wrong Relationship. That way, when the guy turned out to be Mr. Wrong for me, not only could I be the abandoner, but also it was obvious to everyone why I left the relationship. No blame.

Rescript: Act Two

> *Your chances of success in any undertaking can always be measured by your belief in yourself.*
> —**Robert Collier**

The second traumatic experience occurs in your preteen or teen years, which may not be so much of a drama as a story arc.

> For Patricia, a financial executive and 57-year-old single mom of three, it was observing her beautiful mother. With little formal education she acquired few skills in life to support

herself and thus relied on her ability to attract a man as her financial stability.

She explained that her mother's bedroom became a merry-go-round of unfulfilling relationships with men willing to take in her and her children. These surrogate fathers frequently turned out to be less than the cream of the crop. Her mom ultimately had four children with four different men. Patricia was the oldest, and because of the constant upheaval at home, she became close to her grandmother. Grandma would give Patricia a silver dollar for every A she earned in school and told her that if she studied hard, she'd succeed. Consequently Patricia grew up believing that pretty brought pain, but smarts made you money. Admittedly, her life was about not "needing" anybody. She said that she'd recently had a conversation with a friend who is a stay-at-home wife. She asked if Patricia wanted her to find a man who would take care of her. How much would it cost? was Patricia's first thought. Giving up control of her own life was not an option for her—she said, "I don't want to be in the position of worrying about how others would take care of me."

Determined to never become beholden to any man, Patricia became the caretaker for every man in her life. She consistently chose to be in relationships with needy men she definitively could not depend on: two ex-husbands and her current boyfriend. Oh, and by the way, she bore three children—all boys! Patricia is a brilliant businesswoman. She works hard and bears the financial burden of her family.

Rescript: Act Three

*Don't change other people. Be the
change you wish to see in other people.*
—**Gandhi**

For single moms, the third life changer is the divorce or death of a spouse. Many women get so lost in their marriages by living in the shadow of their spouses that they completely lose their entire identities.

Kate, a lawyer and 42-year-old single mom of two, shared her seminal life-changing moment with me. Kate was 18 when she met her husband, and by the time she reached 21 years old, they were married. Her 42nd birthday was the first one as a single adult. Because she wasn't married anymore, she decided to go to Hawaii with her sister and a friend. They had rented a condo so that they could come and go as they pleased and have meals without going to a restaurant all the time. Kate volunteered to do the food shopping. She went to the grocery store by herself. "So there I was, standing in the produce section between the Honeycrisps and the Fuji apples when it suddenly struck me: What kind of apples do I like? I was so used to shopping for everyone else I had no idea what I wanted," she said. "I stood in the produce section crying because I didn't know what to pick."

Kate's advice is to take the time to figure out what you want. Then, the next time you get into a relationship, you will know who "you" are before you become a "them."

20/20 Rescript

The good news is that it's never too late to put heart back into one's life.
—Lucia Capacchione

Take time to sit down with a blank journal and rescript your back story. Write everything about your past and how you would like to tell that story. Then you can begin to map out a direction for your future. Write about who you want to be, where you see your life going, and how you would like it to play out. The more concrete you can be, the better. In my spiritual psychology program, it is called a living vision. Don't worry if your life shifts—you can always modify or update it as you go. After all, it is *your* living vision!

With fortitude and commitment to the new choices, your rescripted story is attainable. Inside all of us, we have what it takes to persevere and succeed.

To love oneself is the beginning of a life-long romance.
—Oscar Wilde

2

FILL
YOUR GLASS

Your grass IS green.
—**Kerri Zane**

"Is your glass half empty or half full?" This is a common expression used to determine if you are an optimist or a pessimist. Any situation can be seen from many angles, and you need to decide in which half of the glass your personal worldview resides.

According to Dr. Martin Seligman, author of *Learned Optimism: How to Change Your Mind and Your Life*, pessimists tend to believe that difficult events will last a long time. This undermines everything they do, and they believe it's entirely their fault. Optimists confronted with hard knocks think of misfortune in the opposite way. They tend to believe that defeat is just a temporary setback confined to one case. They do not believe that defeat is their fault but is rather a challenge to learn from and then try harder the next time.

How do you see your life post divorce? Will it be the glass-half-empty type in which you trudge through the rest of it with your proverbial load of baggage? Or will you be a glass-half-full woman and view your previous relationship as an invaluable lesson in the game of life. Your answer to this question has implications for how your post-marital years will play out. It will drive your actions in every interaction of your future relationships with your children, former mate, and future REAL One. The closer to the brim of your champagne flute you go, the more you will thrive!

Put The Head Chatter On Hold

There is only one meaning of life: the act of living itself.
—Erich Fromm

To get the glass half full, you must start by eliminating your negative thought process. Everyone has voices inside his or her head chattering at him or her all the time. It can't be helped. Sit quietly for the next 60 seconds. Are you watching the second hand sweep by? Can you hear those inhabiters of your awareness yakking away? They're probably asking you why you are sitting quietly listening to them right now, and they're also undoubtedly commenting on how stupid it must feel. In any event, those voices are talking to you constantly. It's okay—you can't stop them, so don't even try. You can, however, rescript their dialogue. If you don't, they are going to keep you living in a state of self-doubt, which will become your pervasive aura. Everyone around you will sense your lack of self-assurance.

Rachel, a 38-year-old stay-at-home single mom of one, went on her first date several months after being separated. She was a nervous wreck about every detail. After the polite introductions Rachel immediately started blabbing about the sweater she was wearing, how old it was, why her soon-to-be ex gave it to her, and how awkward that was. Then, she launched into why her relationship fell apart. She knew what was spilling out of her mouth, and she knew it wasn't appropriate first-date talk. She said, "I was listening to myself and listening to the voices in my head—it was never-ending gibberish. I was trying to cut through it all to listen to him, but it wasn't happening. I was exhausted and confused. Then, I heard the final voice announce, 'You are a stupid woman!' I ended up feeling as if *I* wouldn't even want to date me, let alone this cute guy sitting across the table from me. I never heard from him again."

For many of us, the most common negative messages that the voices repeat over and over include *you're so stupid, you're a loser, you never do anything right, why would anyone ever like you?* Or, *you're such a klutz.* The messages tend to imagine the worst in everything, especially you. If you acknowledge the voices enough, over time, you'll start to believe what they're saying no matter how untrue or unreal they are. Loving yourself first begins when you can replace the negative-message head chatter with new positive internal personal perspectives.

Erase The Head Hate: Step One

Start to really focus on your head chatter. When one of the negative thoughts pops into your head, stop the process as soon as you realize what's going on. Then ask yourself the following questions about these mental misfits:

- Is this message really true?
- Would my friend say this to another person about me? If she wouldn't, why am I?
- What do I gain out of thinking this thought?

Erase The Head Hate: Step Two

Turn the negatives into positives. Science has discovered that you can only keep one thought in your head at a time. Your job is to opt for the happy thought rather than the negative one. You can begin to rescript the self-deprecating behavior through deleting negative words like *worried, frightened, upset, tired, bored, not, never* and *can't* from your chatterbox vocab by planting positive ones like *happy, peaceful, loving, enthusiastic, warm,* and *can.* Don't allow statements like *I'm scared that…, I'm upset because…,* or *It worries me if…* to rule your internal dialogues. Instead, substitute a statement like *It will be nice when….* Always use the present tense, e.g., *I am healthy, I am well,* and *I am happy.* Start your statement with *I, me,* or your own name. Positive present-tense head chatter allows your upbeat mindset to already exist. Also, by using the personal pronoun, it gives you true ownership. Shifting your head chatter from a tenuous state of *what-ifs* or *when this…then that* to the proactive *I ams* will help you to manifest your goals.

Marcy recently learned the power of living in the positive when her husband of 15 years moved out of their family home and, simultaneously, her business that had been flourishing for 25 years was hit hard by a downturn. The negative head chatter could have rocked her world, but this 54-year-old single mom of two teenage daughters shut the voices down as soon as the decibels started to rise.

"My only choice was to keep moving forward," she said. "It's burdensome to worry about a future I have no control over." Marcy had to constantly remind herself to forget about the *what ifs* and keep putting one foot in front of the other— otherwise, she'd become frozen and unable to take care of her kids and herself. She went to that *I am* space and saw herself in a better financial position. She made some calls and got an interview. Marcy completely changed her career. She now has a good job with a comfortable salary and benefits. The best part? She no longer needs to worry about relying on her ex's financial help—or anyone's help, for that matter.

Marcy's world went from a shaky uncertainty to certain assuredness.

Like Marcy, once you learn to concentrate on what you want to accomplish rather than on what you do not want to occur, your glass will begin to fill. In fact, psychological research shows that people who focus on positive experiences are able to put up with more discomfort than negative-thinking people. This mind-over-matter capability is an invaluable tool.

Put Your Smile On

> *The truth is, life really is a matter of how you look at it.*
> —**Martin Seligman**

Smiles have powerful healing capabilities. Again, science has shown that putting on your happy face influences your brain to respond in a positive way. In one study, subjects who were asked to hold a pen in their mouths, which caused them to inadvertently make the facial muscle movements characteristic of a smile, rated cartoons to be funnier than did the other subjects even though they were unaware that it was their own smile that was boosting their reaction. The biological reason for this is that when you feel down, your brain tells your face you're sad, and your facial muscles respond by putting on a depressed expression. This reflects back to your head that yes, in fact, you're feeling blue. By consciously changing your facial muscles so they don't correspond to what you're feeling, you send a different message to your head. The brain will respond by beginning to change your mood accordingly. Are you smiling yet?

Forty-six-year-old Regina, a longtime single mom of two daughters and recent grandma, has seen firsthand the power of singularly sensational solo thoughts.

When her youngest daughter got pregnant at 19 years old, Regina was angry with her. They never had a solid foundation, and this new wrinkle really put a strain on their relationship. "I became one of those people I don't like," Regina told me. "*I didn't even want to be around my sad face all the time.*" Her daughter's decision to have children at such a young age upset her so much that it was affecting her own life. Then she realized that she couldn't live her daughter's life or expect her daughter to live her life the way Regina thought she should. When Regina was able to focus solely on her daughter's happiness and observe what a good mother she was, her whole demeanor changed. Regina said, "I didn't say a word, but just smiled with her. I began to really enjoy spending time with my grandchildren. My daughter started smiling back, and of course, the babies have beautiful smiles."

Regina's happy thought processes helped her find a world worth smiling about.

Bestpectation

> *Any fact facing us is not as important as our attitude*
> *toward it, for that determines our success or failure.*
> —**Norman Vincent Peale**

As you begin your day, your frame of mind proves extremely important. If you start your day in the positive and expect that you will succeed in completing what you set out to do, you exponentially increase the chances that you will have a successful outcome. It's a "bestpectation"—expecting the best possible outcome in every circumstance. A bestpectationer is able to look at the bright side of life so that even the darkest of situations can be spun into golden opportunities.

Sue told me her glass-half-full perspective comes in the form of "magic phone calls." Your life can feel ho-hum and sad until suddenly you get that call, e-mail, text, or IM that spins your life around 180 degrees.

When Sue's golden retriever, Dora, was diagnosed with cancer, she had no idea how she was going to find the $1,200 to pay for the treatment. Just after Dora's first appointment, Sue pulled her car into a busy parking lot to run an errand. Outside, pandemonium suddenly broke out. A car had backed into Sue's car, leaving a noticeable door ding. The following day, the adjuster came to inspect the damage and estimated it to be around $1,000. Sue's magic phone call came when the adjuster realized he'd underestimated the cost of the damage. Instead of $1,000, Sue received a $1,200 check. It was exactly the dollar amount needed to pay Dora's vet bill, and since the car was not a life-or-death situation, she saved that repair for later.

Sue believes you can't stress out about the things that you can't change. Inevitably—and yes, even magically—with positive thinking, everything works out.

Like Sue, when you keep an optimistic view of the world, you will magically draw in people and opportunities that prove helpful. This upbeat attitude can apply to all aspects of your life, both business and personal. So, once you have your living vision for your REAL One, he will show up. Expect the best for you, and you will get exactly what you expect. That's bestpectation!

Commit To You

Some people talk about what they're going to
do, others do what they're talking about.
—Michael Rosenthal

If you believe in yourself and what you are doing, you can accomplish anything. The people who make things happen are the ones who feel a profound sense of mission. They see situations not as problems but simply situations that they can process through to a resolution. The best way to develop positivity is for you to project your success several times a day, every day. Think about what you want and specifically what you need to do to get it. It is often helpful to set your intentions in the morning before you get up out of bed and again before you go to sleep. Intentions are clearly articulated thoughts that you can say aloud or to yourself in the present tense. Your intense focus on what you want will reprogram your mind for the perfect rescript.

For example: *I am joyfully opening my heart to welcome The REAL One into my life.* I write my intentions on 4 x 6 cards and keep them next to my toothbrush so that I can read them at least twice a day. Or you may want to create a visual representation with a collage, using cutout pictures and words you find in magazines.

After one failed marriage, Tessa, a 64-year-old therapist and former single mom of one, knows that when you set your sights on what you want, you are sure to get your heart's desire. This positive perspective helped her find her soul mate. Tessa told me that when she first met her now-husband of 30 years, the only thing she forgot to put on her REAL One intention list was that he be geographically desirable! They lived 300 miles apart.

Happy-Meter Measures

Happiness is a choice, not an automatic response.
—**Mildred Barthel**

Some people have the mindset of thinking that just because they are living and breathing amongst us on the planet, humongously wonderful experiences should be deposited into their happiness bank on a daily basis. As much as I would love for that to be the case, the reality is that you've got to meet the happy meter halfway. It's important to take stock of your big and little joys and appreciate them all, especially when you're feeling sucker-punched by divorce. It's only when you start to look at *all* the good things that you gain perspective on the so-called bad things.

The best example of this way of life is Dori, a 42-year-old five-time stage-four cancer survivor and single mother to an autistic teenage daughter. Anyone would look at what Dori has endured in her life and think that this woman received more than her fair share of reasons to not wake up happy in the a.m. Yet at every turn, rather than viewing her life as a tale of dismay, she found joy in not just surviving but thriving.

Dori shared that she has been through relationships that have left her emotionally bankrupt, but she survived. She has lost loved ones and survived. She grieved the loss of her 14-year marriage and survived. Through all of it, her daughter has been her silver lining. "My daughter is my reason for getting up out of bed every morning," Dori said. "I know she needs me, and I needed to be needed. "Every day is a gift to me and a gift I get to share with others."

Any one of Dori's circumstances could have taken her or anyone else into a glass-half-empty tailspin. Her saving grace was her ability to define each of these events in a new way.

Take a moment to think about what you've overcome and consider it an accomplishment. You survived your divorce. You steeled yourself as you grieved the death of a loved one. And you are making your way in the world step by step. Wake up every morning and remind yourself of all the things you have to be thankful for.

Take pride in your accomplishments, and project yourself happily into your next successful REALationship.

Happy Helpers

Happiness is like a kiss...you must share it to enjoy it.
—Bernard Meltzer

Everyone knows someone who is predominantly a pessimist. His or her goal is to rally the troops over to the "dark side." Don't let it happen. People who embody negative energy and always see the losing side of a situation will eventually bring out the doubt and negativity in you. Minimize or eliminate these people from your inner sanctum, and instead surround yourself with kind, generous, and upbeat glass-half-full people.

There is no question that merely watching others around you as they engage in random acts of kindness will create a significant boost to your mood and increase your own desire to perform a good deed as well. You know you've felt it, like when someone compliments you on your shoes or your new hairstyle and you feel compelled to return the compliment. Or rather than taking your lunch leftovers home with you, you box them up to share with a less-fortunate individual.

These words and actions boost the positive energy in someone else's life and send your serotonin level soaring. Research shows that there is a 60 percent decrease in mortality among people who help others—it's the happy condition called the "helper's high." So, no matter how down in the dumps divorce takes you, daily life will present an opportunity to say or do something kind, generous, and genuine for another. By not asking for credit or recognition, you will gain a greater sense of satisfaction.

> Debbie, a marketing executive and 46-year-old single mother of two, relied heavily on her happy-go-lucky friends to get her through the dark days.
>
> Debbie described herself as a person who has just been able to mentally skip through life in spite of the many bumps in her road. The list was long. She was abused as a child, her parents divorced, her dad passed away, and then she became a teen mom. At 25, she met a new man and became pregnant again, but the guy cheated on her (while Debbie was pregnant). Debbie kicked him out. Then, her son was born with cerebral palsy. He's almost 15 years old now and confined to a wheelchair. Life has been a series of incredible challenges for Debbie, but through it all, her strong faith in God and her upbeat happy friends have sustained her. "I take my responsibilities seriously, but I don't carry my burdens with me or hang them on anyone else," Debbie told me. "Some people like to focus on the hard parts—the negatives of life. I had to learn to eliminate those people from my world. I chose to be around the happy ones."

24/7 Bliss

Go to your happy place, go to your happy place, go to your happy place.
—Sue Steinberg

Of course, even the most positive person in the world isn't happy all the time, nor should that be the goal. We race through our daily to-do lists without being in the moment of our day-to-day experiences. We forget to stop and notice the little things that make us smile or truly listen to those around us. We forget to visit our daily "happy place." Your happy place is a state of mind, a tranquil place that calms you down and allows you to restore balance. It's kind of like a mental vacation spot. It's a time and space for you to be alone with your thoughts and is also a phenomenal coping tool. When things happen that throw you off balance, like a loss or an argument, going to your happy place will help you refocus your energy. It literally activates your internal healing process through visualization, self-hypnosis, and a repetitive meditative process.

You can also choose to engage in peaceful activities like taking a walk at the beach, strolling around a lake, hiking up a mountain to take in the beautiful vistas, meandering through a field full of flowers, or exercising. The expression *runner's high* does not infer an addiction but a feeling or a state of euphoria. There are also simple around-the-house activities that allow you to be in your head and refocus your center: baking, gardening, or, as weird as it sounds, vacuuming. Everyone's happy place is different.

Imagine A Bright Future

When I look into the future, it's so bright it burns my eyes.
—Oprah Winfrey

The pursuit of goals in your personal life, your relationships, or your career is the difference between having a mediocre life or a life full of passion and enthusiasm. The absence of purpose in your life—or more specifically, avoiding the pursuit of your goals—will make you feel stuck and unaccomplished.

In a study conducted at New York University, scientists found that humans actually have the tendency to be optimistic about their future. That's encouraging, isn't it? You expect to live longer, be more successful than average, and less likely to become ill or fall prey to hardship. "When participants imagined positive future events relative to negative ones, enhanced activation was detected in the rostral anterior cingulate and amygdala, which are the same brain areas that seem to malfunction in depression," said researcher Tali Sharot. The team found that participants were more likely to expect positive events than negative ones to happen closer in the future and to imagine them with greater vividness. Ah, the power of positive thinking!

Allyson, a 27-year-old publicist and single mother of one son, is the consummate bright-future lady. Allyson was five months pregnant when her son's father peaced out. "I always figured I'd be a single mom, but I didn't think I would be where I was when it happened," she said. Allyson had a vision of how she wanted to care for herself and her child. It was time to pull her life together. She moved to a new city and started working at a public relations firm. Today her career is flourishing. She told me, "Only the serious ones can laugh." In other words, only people who are serious about moving on in their life can shrug off a bad situation and keep on going. Now, with her life back on track, she said she's open to including a man in her world. "There is some guy out there who will be a wonderful addendum to my life. I know it!" she exclaimed.

For Allyson, finding her REAL One is a perfectly legitimate next step to having a completely glass-half-full life.

Simply living in the optimistic belief that you will find the perfect partner can be the secret ingredient to ultimately achieving a contented personal life.

> *Live out your imagination, not your history.*
> **—Steven Covey**

3 FLYING IN THE FACE OF FEAR

If you never try, you will never fail. If you never fail, you never will be fearless.
—Kerri Zane

Fear. This is a biggie! We all face fears, both small and large, every day. It is human nature to fear—it is what many times drive us to make the choices we make. In many ways, our fears can function in a protective way. Like, don't go out with another bad boy again— you know you're gonna get your heart broken. Or, are you really going to give the alcoholic one more chance? Really?

Fear can also stifle our accomplishments. It's the number-one barrier to living audaciously and having the life you've truly imagined for yourself. It's one of the main reasons women can see their glasses as half empty. Fear tells you to not put yourself out there in the universe on a dating site or to stay home from a party because you are afraid of strangers. But people you don't know are strangers until you meet them, no matter how you meet them. Then, they aren't strangers anymore.

In other words, fear operates when you don't do something you want to do, or conversely, when you do something you don't want to do. Bottom line: Fear is the little demon that sits on your shoulder holding you back from growth, success, fulfillment and happiness.

Before embarking on your journey to find your REAL One, you need to learn how to not get stuck in fear's defensive position. *Fight, flight, or frozen* are fear's triple-F threat that keep you from being able to work things out in comfortable ways and move forward confidently with your life and into a new REALationship.

The Physical Functions Of Fear

No one can make you feel inferior without your consent.
—Eleanor Roosevelt

Fear is not just a psychological response to situations—there are physiological implications as well. This explains why it's not easy to overcome, but it is possible! When you get scared or anxious or highly stressed, the amygdala (the part of our brain that processes emotion and memories) activates your body's fear circuits, which increases heart rate and blood pressure. Your palms get sweaty, and your mouth gets dry and your muscles tense. In cavewoman time, this allowed us to be at the ready to flee in fear or stand in fight when faced with a scary mammal. Very useful then—now, not so much. Fearful reactions are not pretty, and with nowhere to flee in your adult life, your fears become ingrained psychodramas that play out repeatedly in your body and brain. This is not healthy!

Single moms face various fears: fading beauty, aging, isolation, rejection, empty nests, loss of financial security, change, death, illness, accidents, and losing a loved one. Things like making decisions, changing careers, making friends, ending or beginning relationships, asserting oneself, losing weight, making a mistake, being successful, experiencing failure, being vulnerable, being conned or helpless, and fear of intimacy loom large!

Sarah is the middle child in a family of three. Her self-absorbed parents paid little attention to her and gave her absolutely no positive reinforcement. After 11 years of living together, Sarah's only long-term relationship came to an abrupt end. She felt the sting of rejection once again. That was almost 15 years ago, and Sarah has not dated since. Why? Fear of rejection.

Lindy married a beautifully handsome man. They had two daughters and a sweet little home in a quaint neighborhood. They both worked very hard, but Lindy's husband had a dark secret: he'd disappear for days on drug and alcohol binges. Lindy tried to help, staying in her marriage for much longer than she should have. Why? Fear of being on her own.

Melissa's dad was never around when her mother needed him. A very successful surgeon, he was always either in his office, in the operating room, or on the lecture circuit. Melissa's mother was very unhappy, but she never had a job or earned her own money, so she was beholden to her husband. Melissa never wanted to live her mother's life, so she got into relationships with weak men. Why? Fear of being vulnerable.

Susan Jeffers, PhD, the author of *Feel the Fear and Do It Anyway,* is a master of helping to guide readers from a place of paralysis to power. "Fears arise from events or situations that haven't happened or may never happen," Jeffers says in her book. "They surface from…thinking patterns…we've created and become adjusted to believing. They evolve from false beliefs we've come to embody over time and then reinforced by outside influences." The messages come from parents who tell you "you're stupid" or "you'll never amount to anything," to spouses who convince you that you would be nothing without them, or bosses who demean your capabilities. These messages are all actually unfounded tapes and, much like your childhood stories, need rescripting. They live inside your head and metastasize; feeding the part of you that is the frightened child wanting safety and comfort.

Sometimes, fear is about overcoming fear. You don't want to succeed because it requires so much, and of course, you might fail. At the bottom of all fears is simply the fear that you can't handle whatever life dishes out. That is simply not true. You've been through at least one marriage and survived. You may have weathered the death of a loved one, an illness, or ailing parents—and don't forget algebra homework. For goodness sake, you survived childbirth—nothing is more fear inducing or painful than that!

Ten years after losing her husband to cancer, Alison, a 48-year-old single mom of one, had to come to terms with her fear-inducing demon, the Grim Reaper. Alison told me she had a great fear of losing anyone she loved. Before she agreed to marry her new husband, she had to come to grips with the fear that there would be a 50 percent chance he would leave her first. She thought about how it would plummet her into the darkness, despair, and hopelessness she'd felt before. She could have allowed her fears to paralyze her and let life pass her by. She realized that would also entail the potential loss of a wonderful relationship. So she compared being alone with having a partner again. He won. Alison chose to look at her fear as false evidence appearing to be real. Now she sees a loved one's death as the time for her to say goodbye rather than as a loss. A happily married woman, she has great joy in the partnership she shares with her new husband.

Just like Alison, your ability to alter your belief in you and the untenable nature of your situation will give you the strength to handle anything that comes your way. It is time to stop wishing your life were different and fearlessly embrace your new circumstances as opportunities for growth and learning.

Fear Truisms

Life is a process of becoming a combination of states we have to go through. Where people fail is that they wish to elect a state and remain in it. This is a kind of death.
—**Anais Nin**

In her book, Jeffers outlines five basic truths about every fear. If you can embrace these truisms, you can then ultimately get to a place where you will feel safe enough to face fear head-on.

First, fear will never go away as long as you continue to grow. Every time you are faced with a new risk or opportunity, there will be the possibility of fear attached to the experience. Second, fear is uncomfortable, and we'd rather do just about anything to avoid it. Fortunately, fear is temporary. Unfortunately, the only way you will know that is to go out and do something scary. Once you move through the fear, it dissipates. Third, the only way to feel better about you is to go out…and do it. Once you do something you've feared, the attachment is gone. You will be so proud of yourself! Fourth, you're not the only one who experiences fear when in unfamiliar territory—everyone else does, too. This is an amazing revelation. If you think that other people have it easy, think again. They are just as frightened about taking those unfamiliar steps as you are. Finally, the reality is that pushing through the fear is less frightening than living with the underlying fear that comes from a feeling of helplessness.

Jeri, a twice-divorced 42-year-old single mom of four, learned that living in limbo, unhappiness, or defeat is much more challenging than taking the leap. When she was 19 years old, she met her first husband. They had three children pretty quickly, but the relationship lacked warmth and a real connection. The longer she lived in her loveless marriage, the more she realized that the children were his control tools. He would frequently tell her that she was spoiled and no other man would want a woman who had three children. She felt physically, verbally, and emotionally abused. She became desperate to find a way out, but told me that he would gaslight her with ploys like disconnecting the starter to her car so she couldn't leave. Finally, the day OJ Simpson went to trial for the murder of his wife, Jeri got the nerve to walk away.

Her second husband came from an incredibly powerful and wealthy family. Her life quickly became not her own again. The money and power were used as aphrodisiacs of control. After only a few years and one more child, Jeri walked away from her life of private jets, hilltop mansions and European holidays. Now she lives in a simple two-bedroom apartment in the flatlands. But she's at peace, because it's hers.

Jeri pushed past the fear of not having money. "Money doesn't measure success—success is measured in pride," she said. Jeri has her pride back. No longer in fear of living "without," she knows that if and when she gets married again, she will not settle; her guy will have to appreciate who she is and what she brings to the table.

One Foot In Front Of The Next

No matter the outcome of your choice, you are not a failure if you don't achieve all that you set out to do. You are a success because you tried!
—Anonymous

Taking the first step is always—yep—the scariest, but knowledge is power and bravery. You don't have to face all your fears head-on all at once.

Monica was a 43-year-old stay-at-home mother of two children when her husband left her. She took her power back by choosing to transform the fear of being left into an opportunity to return to loving herself as a "me" instead of a "we."

"Whether you leave your marriage or you've been left, there is inherent fear," she said. Monica is a devout Catholic, so when her husband chose to leave, everything she believed in was completely shattered. "When you are that broken, you become incapacitated," she said. "My world was a blank page, and I had no idea how to fill it. I could have stayed locked in my room for the rest of my life or faced everything in life fearlessly." She believed that God would bring her the signs that she needed, and she got tremendous support from her friends. Life for Monica was one minute at a time and then one day at a time until she finally felt as if she could face every fear. She chose to stay open to every experience; rather than wallow in thoughts of failure or mistake, she saw the end results as lessons. She became very aware of all the information being thrown at her and became a sponge, relearning how to live as an independent woman.

Monica created her no-fear game plan, and so can you. Small steps are easier to accomplish. It was a long road for her, but had she not taken the first step, she would have continued to live frozen in her unhappiness. Each step accomplished encourages the next step. Rescripting your living vision will keep you from veering off in directions that don't support who you really are or who you want to be. Look for people whose lives you want to emulate. Watch what they do and how they do it. Ask for their help and guidance. You don't have to face your fears solo.

Taking Charge Of You

You are the sole proprietor of your happy switch, so go ahead flip it on!
—Kerri Zane

When a difficult situation presents itself, write down all the possible ways you can feel about it. Change your vocabulary from *I can't* to *I won't, I should* to *I could, It's not my fault* to *I'm totally responsible, It's a problem* to *It's an opportunity, I'm never satisfied* to *I want to learn more, Life is a struggle* to *Life is an adventure, I hope* to *I know, If only* to *Next time, What will I do* to *I know I can handle it* and *It's terrible* to *It's a learning experience.* By considering alternative outcomes, the fearful situation is rescripted into a condition of choice, and thus the fear is mitigated.

It's much easier to take responsibility for choosing your path and going into a situation knowing that it's not so much a frightening unknown but rather a conscious choice. No matter what your choice, it is neither right nor wrong—it is simply yours. If an endeavor doesn't turn out exactly as you planned, take comfort in knowing that you've just learned a new lesson and uncovered new paths to explore. You will see that when you start to make your own choices, you are in control of your own destiny. You have the choice to change anything about yourself that you desire. Do not fear the twists and turns of life; know that they exist, and watch for signs to recalibrate. Follow where life leads you—it may be more fun than what you had planned.

Cece was a 56-year-old executive and mother of two teens. She had been married for 31 years when her husband asked for a divorce. She was devastated when it happened and frightened at the prospect of being the sole provider.

Cece pulled herself together, took her boys, moved to a new town, and got a job. Her boys are now finishing college, and she proudly told me that she paid for all of it. Her youngest son told her that at first he hated what had happened to their family, but he now appreciates their new life. She realized at that moment that she had shed 200 pounds of useless fat (her former husband). It took her a while, but she said, "I began to recognize that he had been antisocial, jealous, manipulative, and dishonest; by extension, I was reclusive, self-deprecating, and unfulfilled. Slowly, I found I could have friends without his approval, could vacation where I wanted, could wear what I wanted, and could eat foods I enjoyed. I also realized I had been carrying the family all along, financially and emotionally. I live my life now, not an existence in someone's shadow." Cece is a much better—and happier—person. Her sons respect her, and best of all, she likes who she is!

Like Cece, once you can wrap your head around the fact that you get to be in charge of what goes on in your life, you have the power within you to make your life what you want it to be. You will find an amazing sense of peace and freedom. As a self-assured woman, you will be in control of your life, and you will embody the positive energy that draws people to you. In turn, you will be able to begin to open up your heart and become authentic and loving to your REAL One. You don't know unless you try. You can stay small and safe. Or you can live an extraordinary life.

Live With No Regrets

Today, I give myself permission to be greater than my fears.
—Anonymous

The most resounding advice all the single moms I interviewed shared was to live without regrets. The overwhelming belief is that it is far more satisfying to have tried and failed than to not have tried at all. Fear is to regret. Fear is a wasted opportunity. That is how I approach every aspect of my life, including how I found my REAL One. It hasn't always been a smooth path, but it has been an interesting road to travel.

As I've grown older, I have learned one thing for certain: I have this one life, and that's it. I don't get a do-over, so there is no point of living a life in fear. There are things to do, places to see, and possibilities to explore, and I intend to experience every single one of those delicious options. I never want to live in regret.

Be A Grown-Up

Do not fear what other people think of you or what they could potentially think of you, especially if one of the people is your potential lover. Only children live and breathe in need of other people's approval. Instead of a child/parent dynamic, choose to be the other half of an adult-partner relationship. You will be more open and loving to others in your life. It is paradoxical, but the truth is that the less you "need" your man's approval, the more you are able to love him unequivocally. The bottom line is this: *You will never please everyone.* It's not worth sacrificing yourself to accommodate anyone else's thoughts about who you should be or what you should do. If you have to live in second-guess land, you're doomed. Besides, that is not a REALationship.

No one knows the consequences of fearing what a partner will think more than Bettina, a 46-year-old writer and single mother of two. For most of her 15-year marriage, she existed in an isolating verbally abusive relationship. Her ex was a narcissistic A-type personality who ruled the house with a vitriolic tongue. The relationship became more abusive after the birth of her children.

Living with her husband was a bit like *Sleeping with the Enemy*. He didn't want the babies to cry, so she would do whatever she needed to do so he wouldn't hear them. If the saltshaker wasn't properly positioned on the dinner table, he'd blow a gasket. Bettina felt compelled to stay in the marriage because all her friends were married. She thought her family would be embarrassed and upset with her. It wasn't until her brother saw what was going on and told her to get out that she felt released. His support allowed her to push past the fear of leaving and being on her own. She went to New York and detoxed. She said, "When I could finally get onto a subway by myself, my excitement was palpable. I realized I could take care of myself. I felt good about being independent. I mean, it's a little scary and a little exciting all at one time."

Bettina became so consumed by her husband that she completely lost her "self." Not only had she been afraid to be alone but she also became afraid of even the simplest of daily activities. She had to find her way back to standing on her own two feet. It takes practice to live fearlessly. Ultimate success does not come without a price. Practice, repetition, and failure are part of that cost. Prepare to pay, and you will ultimately succeed.

Ok, Just Did It! Now What?

Don't be afraid of making a mistake, be bold for making a choice.
—**Anonymous**

Once you take the leap into the choice, trust yourself and make the commitment to follow your path. After all, it's *your* choice, right? Accept total responsibility for your decision, and stand by your choice. You are no longer the victim or the child; so don't play the blame game. It is much easier to accept the responsibility for making your choice if you stand by your conviction. Whatever you do, don't look back. The key to success is to keep the flow and momentum moving forward. If, after a time, you find yourself falling back into the fear zone, start your writing process of listing opportunities and alternate endings. Don't like what you see? Don't get stuck—you have the right to make another choice. This is *your* life, and you've only got one shot.

My mother told me this story that literally altered the course of my life. Armin was my dad's cousin. He was a sweet man who married young and had two daughters. Shortly after Armin married his wife, it became apparent to him that she was ill. She had a mental disorder that slowly revealed itself as she aged and sadly manifested in both of his daughters. This beautiful man lived a tortured life with three mentally ill women. Toward the end of his life, he'd contracted a heart disease. His doctors told him death was imminent. Just before he passed away, Armin declared, "I have lived my whole life in a miserable marriage, and now I am going to die". That is how this angel of a man summed up his life. My mother related this story to me as I was struggling in my marriage. Armin helped me face my fear. I did not want to spend the rest of my life unhappy like Armin and die regretting not having taken the risk at finding contentment.

'Yes' Is Your Only Answer

As Dr. Jeffers outlines so deftly in *Feel the Fear and Do It Anyway*, "saying yes is the antidote to fear." This is not limited to regarding the acts of dealing with just the day-to-day disappointments, rejections, and missed opportunities—it is the miracle tool for dealing with our deepest, darkest fears. With a glass-half-full positive attitude, every choice is possible. Saying yes means acting on your belief that you can create meaning and purpose in whatever life hands you. It means channeling resources to find constructive, healthy ways to deal with adverse situations. It means acting out of strength, not weakness. Say yes to your universe.

> *Some people want it to happen, some wish*
> *it would happen, others make it happen.*
> —Michael Jordan

4 BEING "ME"

Authenticity occurs when the head and the heart
meet at the lips; when what we think and what
we feel is congruent with what we say and do.
—Dr. Carl Hammerschlag

Women = People Pleasers. Accommodators. Pushovers...Stop the madness, *now*!

We want everyone to like us, we want to get along, and we want peace. At a young age, women learn to accommodate parents, teachers and, later in life, bosses and spouses. We are taught that in order to have our needs met, we need to play by other peoples' rules. We are "good girls" because we go along with the program. Then slowly, as the years pass, we wake up and realize that this habit of always making everything okay for everyone else doesn't work for us anymore. The daily compromises chip away at our self-worth until we don't know who "being me" is anymore. It finally plays havoc with our internal harmony—we find that we don't want to subjugate ourselves anymore. Similarly, in many cases, our spouses become annoyed as we shift behavior and grow out of being subservient. In either case, there is a good chance the marriage bond will break. But the silver lining of uncoupling is that it allows us to peel back the marital layers and rediscover the inner beauty of what *being me* truly means.

> When I was married with small children, everyone else's needs and desires came before mine. One day, I was out to lunch with a friend, confidante, and trusted advisor, and she randomly, it seemed, asked me, "What kind of eggs do you like?" What the heck is she talking about? I thought. We're having lunch, not breakfast. And I'm not that fond of eggs anyway. Clearly, I didn't understand the question. Then she explained. There's a classic scene at the end of the movie *The Runaway Bride,* where Ike (Richard Gere) asks Maggie (Julia Roberts) what kind of eggs she likes. Up until that point, Maggie would eat whichever eggs her fiancé liked without regard for what it was that she herself liked. It was a pivotal moment for the character in the film and a metaphor for her life. It is at that second that her authenticity began.

Living my authenticity, or "being me," was not how I functioned back then. Like many of the other now-single moms I have interviewed, we make the lion's share of compromises to keep marriages whole.

> Hayley is a recently divorced 42-year-old single mom of three. After nearly 13 years of being with her husband, she realized that because she had not been true to herself at the start of her

relationship she'd ultimately lost all of herself. She told me that she'd known from the beginning that the chemistry was just not there. He made a full-court press; wooing her with all the material things money could buy. She agreed to marry him but knew she was settling for less than what she truly wanted.

"I literally had a conscious conversation with myself about what I was about to commit to," she told me. Before she was married, she had enjoyed a very active sex life. After she was married, she'd have sex once a month and an orgasm maybe twice a year. It was very unsatisfying for her. She told me she tried to teach her husband how to please her, but he didn't care enough. She resigned herself to the fact that the trade-off for passion was a comfortable life for her children.

Then, last year, she met a guy. She's not sure what possessed her to give the guy her number, but she did. They spent two amazing nights together. Eventually, her husband found out. Consequently, their relationship became very toxic. What Hayley realized was that the affair wasn't about sex, it was a wake-up call. She'd been living in an empty cash-filled fog her entire marriage. It was time to start living her truth.

Hayley's strongest first step was realizing that by buying into someone else's agenda, she was depriving herself of all the inner and outer body nourishment she needed. In order to have another chance at true love, Hayley and the rest of us need to live authentically and express our core needs, wants, and beliefs peacefully, but without compromise from the outset of a new relationship. How does one do that? As Hayley said, it starts with sharing your truth.

Your Truth Is Not *The* Truth

> *Don't compromise yourself. You're all you've got.*
> — Janis Joplin

To transition out of your old ways and into the "being me" that will attract your new REALationship takes some serious self-reflection and understanding the distinction between YOUR truth and THE truth. THE truth is subjective and is each individual's personal perspective. In other words, it's a "he said, she said" sort of scenario. There is a no more visceral he-said-she-said than what happens at the end of a marriage. The how and why of what started out to be such a magically perfect union gets torn apart at the seams as the finger pointing escalates to a fever pitch. Each individual's interpretation of the events plays out from only his or her point of view.

MY truth and YOUR truth are the truths that are undeniable. It is who you are, who you want to be, and how you want people to see you. In other words, it is your authentic self. The authentic self is the real you; it is what you think and how you feel. YOUR truth is the place where self-esteem, compassion, understanding, insight, forgiveness, and intuition live. When you have complete clarity about your truth, then you can represent who you are to the world and, of course, to your new prospective REAL One.

Listen To Your Intuition

> *My truth is truthfully the only truth that matters.*
> — Kerri Zane

The best way to get to the core of your truth is to listen to your inner voice, aka your intuition. They are the new ideas and new goals that allow you a better way to live. Your intuition is always clear. It will encourage you to come out from behind the mask of settling or making do and allow yourself to genuinely live your integrity.

Marilyn, an investment banker and 50-year-old single mother of two, ignored her intuition and entered into an inevitably doomed second marriage.

"There were so many red flags I simply ignored," she said. They'd just started dating about three months when she got a promotion. He didn't want her to take the job. In spite of his resistance, she did it anyway, but not until after they'd had a huge fight about it. Then, one night, they were playing a game at home with her kids. He thought the kids were cheating and got upset. "I so wanted the relationship to work," she recalled. "I justified his behavior by rationalizing that he was an intense guy and very cerebral." She just thought he needed some training and he would be okay. She told me that the kids felt uncomfortable with him, but they sucked it up for mom. They wanted her to be happy. "Honestly, can you imagine a grown guy getting worked up about something like that?" she said. "Before I knew it, we were living together and he asked me to marry him. He got down on his knee, and I remember that I was literally shaking my head no. Everything in my being was saying no. I had a flash: What would happen if I had to divorce him? What would the emotional cost be? But then, I just figured that my kids needed a dad and he could take care of me." Before she knew it, Marilyn was in too deep.

Homage to your Adjectives

Now it is your turn. Use your intuition as your guide. Think about what you can legitimately change about yourself or your current situation. Think about the things you love about yourself. It might be helpful for you to create a "being me" outline. Identify what the inner qualities, values, beliefs, wants, needs, goals, and motivations are that you would like to project out into the universe to bring this brand-new REAL One to you. It's about who you are and what you want rather than who *he* is. Trust that if you put the best you out there, the perfect true love will show up.

Here are a few questions to help get you started. Be super-honest in answering these questions. You are on the path to finding not just any guy—as in anyone—but the REAL One who will honor YOUR truth.

1. *Are you happy with the outer reflection you're presenting to the world?*
2. *Are you at peace with your inner self?*
3. *What are your core beliefs?*
4. *What do you value most in your life?*
5. *What are your top five needs in your life?*
6. *What are your top five wants in your life?*
7. *Does your inner self match how your outer self appears?*
8. *What are the changes you feel you need to make to allow a new lover into your life?*

Carole Brody Fleete, the author of *Widows Wear Stilettos* and the 50-year-old single mom of one daughter, has experienced both divorce and widowhood in her past. With each life challenge, she became very clear about her values, beliefs, wants, and needs. The more comfortable she became in her own skin, the more in sync she became with her core. For her, this meant stretching out of her comfort zone.

Several months after her husband passed away, she bravely decided to take a solo road trip to Las Vegas. By going out and doing things that were a stretch for her, she gave herself the space and time to fine-tune her ability to uncover her true thoughts about who she was and what she wanted. She tells the widows she counsels that when they can find clarity about who they are on the inside, it will allow them to better and more confidently project who they are on the outside with their words and actions. They will find as they go through this self-discovery process that the more definitive they are in their own minds about what is important to them, the stronger they will feel about their convictions and the less likely they will be to yield to external pressures. A woman's biggest downfall is the need to appease and people-please. Sorry, no more Miss Goody Two Shoes! She is gone! Not that any woman should turn into a mean girl, but the old default behavior is going to yield to this new ab-fab Miss Confidence. If you please *you* first, everything else in your life will fall into place exactly the way you want.

Carole said her greatest achievement came when she put herself into that place of "being me." It released her from the underlying feeling that she had to be perfect. She stopped living her life by everyone else's standards and held to her own standard instead. There is an incredible lightness of being that comes with no longer striving to be someone you think your child, mother, father, (potential) significant other, or society wants you to be.

Work on allowing your behavior along with your conversation to be a true and spontaneous expression of your inner feelings with no confusion, misunderstanding, or hurt feelings. Consciously align all your character traits into your values, beliefs and actions. This will become the essence of your integrity; you will say what you mean and mean what you say. If you stick to only committing to what you know, you can deliver and say what is truly in your heart of hearts. It will go a long way toward building trust and respect, which form the foundation for building true love. Of course, it is then incumbent upon you to recognize him. But with a definitive knowing of who you are, your REAL One list will undoubtedly shift. The absolute knowing of your own core characteristics will prepare you for a romantic REALationship.

Marilyn, now separated from that second husband, became clear about what was missing from her REAL One list: HER.

"I moved too quickly from my first marriage into my second—we met and married within six months. What I realize now, though, is that I wasn't looking forward and exploring what I really wanted. I was just looking backward and was really clear about what I didn't want. I ran straight into my new husband. He was the exact opposite of what I had. I thought that was enough. I really didn't take the time to explore who I was or what would be the best next step for me. Next time, it's all about who I am, and then I'll decide who might fit into my life."

The Great Relationship Fake-Out

Life isn't about finding yourself. Life is about creating yourself.
—George Bernard Shaw

Many women (and men, too, for that matter) search for so long to find a relationship that when a potential true love does show up, they do whatever it takes to make it work. Often, this includes being inauthentic—that is, being who you think the other person wants you to be instead of being your real self. This desire to find someone and be accepted and loved at all costs is based on fundamental insecurities. It is the unfounded fear that all the old anguish from your last relationship will resurface in your current relationship if you don't play along with what you think the other person wants. It is the polar opposite of what you should be doing. Unfortunately, that kind of inauthentic way of being is exactly what keeps you from getting to that place of REALationship. Guilty as charged, over and over!

After my marriage, I dated several men, and whatever their passion was became mine, whether I liked it or not. The most egregious loss of authenticity was the time I spent with the engineer—we did four- and five-hour hikes every weekend. Did I love hiking? Not really. But he was tall and handsome and the vision of exactly whom my family and friends thought I should be with. I desperately wanted to make this relationship work. He was not the most scintillating conversationalist, but he was tall and handsome. We never went out to dinner except when I paid for meals, but he was tall and handsome. He was extremely religious, and I'm more of a once-a-year worshipper, but he was tall and handsome. I sank into a cauldron of lies that got so deep I wasn't sure how to get out.

The hiking was wreaking havoc on my hip joints, but I kept on marching up and down the hills. I was desperate to get out of the house for a meal, but sat happily at his dinner table night after night. I couldn't imagine going to prayer week in and week out for the rest of my life, but I donned the waaay too conservative dresses and showed up. The worst fib was the lie about my age. He was three years younger than I was. When I met him, he thought I was two years younger than he. I never corrected him. In fact, I perpetuated the lie with more lies to support the first lie and even recruited my mom to lie about her age. For the three months of that relationship I lived on pins and needles, fearful that he'd discover my real age and my cover would be blown and I'd be exposed as a fraud. It happened. One night at my house, he saw a document with my actual birth date. The ruse was over, and so was the relationship. I was clearly not "being me," and I felt horrible. You get the picture! I let the *tall and handsome* (my short-sighted REAL One list) override my authenticity.

It took a lot of soul searching to come out of that one and realize that I have to speak my truth from now on in every aspect of my life. By not being authentic, I wasted a lot of physical and emotional energy. It was difficult and painful. You can fool some of the people some of the time (even yourself), but not all of the people all of the time.

Andrea, an executive and 50-year-old single mom of two, is a fiercely strong and independent woman who daily lives her authenticity.

"It's not necessarily because I'm prettier than most, but my overall package is nice," she said. "I am smart and attractive. I never ever give my power away. I've never looked for someone else to fix me or complete me. If I'm missing tiles [i.e., roof tiles], they're *mine*. Someone else can enhance my life, but they can't make me *me*. With men, I figure they are either gonna like me or not. If you are independent, it reads as confidence, and men are attracted to confidence. Desperation is like bad breath—no one wants to be within 10 feet of you. When you are positive, there is a light, and men see it."

Like Andrea, when you fashion your life where the decisions you make and the actions you take are well considered, deliberate, and in harmony with what's important to you, you are living an authentic life, and all will flow in a direction that is exquisitely meaningful for you. When your inner and outer worlds are congruent, the pieces fit and everything clicks. If you know at your core that you are living a life that is aligned with your purpose, is filled with what you love, and supports your growth, you are living an authentic life with dignity and self-respect. You will have peace, contentment, and confidence.

One can have no smaller or greater mastery than mastery of oneself.
—Leonardo Da Vinci

5 RIGHT HERE, RIGHT NOW

*Study as if you were to live forever. Live as
if you were going to die tomorrow.*
—St. Isidore of Seville

Mindful Plus *Playful*

Living in the moment is also called *mindfulness*, which is a state of active, open, and intentional attention on the present. Just as you were able to see your story as a story and rescript it, you realize that you are not your thoughts when you become mindful. You become an observer of your thoughts from moment to moment without judging them. It is at the root of Buddhism, Taoism, and many Native-American traditions and it is the essence of yoga and fitness workouts. When you can add a touch of playful to your mindful, your present tense becomes joyful. You are the girl every guy wants to be around.

This could be easier said than done, particularly as a working single mom. When you're on the job, you're thinking about being with your children; when you're at home attending to your children, you worry about the work piling up on your desk. For me, that feeling of never being ahead of the game became overwhelming and oppressive.

I struggled with being mindful for much of my early adulthood. The self-persecution of always needing to be ahead of myself reached a crescendo at age 38. A lot of the nuttiness in my brain was predicated on the looming round-number birthday, the Big 4-0, and my desire to accomplish everything I'd set out to do in my life before I reached that auspicious milestone.

Rather than take pleasure and be present with my young children during their bathtub playtime, I stressed about what I should have been doing at work. It got so bad for me that I recall putting on my makeup one morning and thinking it was a waste of precious ticking clock. As my daughters will tell you, that is weird! I actually enjoy the process of putting on makeup. So this whole waste-of-time thing was driving me insane! I wanted to jump out of my skin.

Instead of letting my life go by without living it—dwelling on intrusive memories of the past or fretting about what may or may not happen in the future—I had to learn to separate the frenetic future pace of my work life with the small pleasures of my everyday personal life. I had to consciously learn to enjoy every moment of my life.

There are no refunds on any of the missed moments in life. They're just gone. *Carpe diem*—seize the day, as the Latin poet

Horace wrote. It's not a new sentiment, but certainly one that we frequently lose sight of especially coming out of situations in which our lives have been wrapped up in taking care of others. It is now your chance to choose: A. You can spend the rest of your life looking ahead or reminiscing about the past; or B. You can revel in the joy you are having in the moment.

This applies to everything in your life: the proud moments, like reaching the peak of a mountain on a hike, buying your first house on your own, or getting a promotion at work. Even the events you construe as chores, like playing chauffeur to your preteens, choosing an outfit and getting dressed in the morning, and yes, even going on yet another online coffee date. None of these is a waste of time but rather a cherished opportunity to be enjoyed!

To be in the here and now every day, takes searching for the stillness and calm. Sounds virtually impossible, doesn't it? But like all good things, it takes practice and intention. A technique I've recently started to use whenever I feel overwhelmed and can't automatically get to my own happy place is to pretend I'm up in plane at 30,000 feet. Up there, the details causing much of my uneasiness disappear, as if I can't see them anymore. It makes me much calmer as I regain a healthy perspective about what is transpiring in my life. If you want it, you can achieve peace in your life.

Be Unselfconscious

When we base our identity on past negatives, we automatically face the present with contracted energy and frozen beliefs that limit healthy new choices.
—Carole Adrienne

To improve your performance on a date or in a social situation, learn to be unselfconsciousness. In other words, stop thinking about it. The irony of living in the moment is that when you think too hard about what you're doing, it actually makes you more anxious. For example, if you're in a situation that makes you uncomfortable, such as introducing yourself to a stranger or flirting at a gathering, clear your mind. Stop obsessing about whether that hot guy at the bar is going to think you're desperate if you engage him in conversation or that whatever spills out of your mouth will be a turnoff. As we learned in Chapter 3, all of these fear-based mind minutiae are wasting valuable energy and making you unnecessarily apprehensive.

Allow everything to unfold as it may. You will be surprised at how much more enjoyable your moment-by-moment experience will be. Situations will become less threatening, and those ugly self-evaluations that you've used so adeptly to beat yourself up with in the past will disappear.

Positive present talk is a skill that 49-year-old Anne, a sales rep and separated single mother of two teens, adeptly learned. She told me that she's taught herself how to consciously be in the *right here, right now* by shifting her vocabulary. "I've eliminated words like *someday I will, I wish, I hope, I CAN'T* and replaced them with *I am* and *I CAN*." Anne was married for almost 20 years. The end of her marriage was a loss, so she allowed herself time to grieve. Then she was done. "It's all in the past now, and I am moving forward with no regrets," Anne said. "I choose to not bring any of my old hope-and-dream language into my new world. Everything for me is in the present. I am a whole lot freer because of it. You can't shift an ocean liner in a swimming pool. I realize that all I want doesn't necessarily happen on my timetable. But I don't let that keep me stuck either. I don't sit still; instead, I take action that keeps me positive and encouraged every day. I don't dream it—I live it."

Master Savoring

Life is a succession of moments. To live each one is to succeed.
—**Corita Kent**

Psychologists define *savoring* as the ability to luxuriate in whatever it is you're doing at the present moment. This could be any activity—taking a walk, watering your garden, or enjoying a kiss. Sonja Lyubomirsky, a psychologist at the University of California, Riverside, and author of *The How of Happiness*, explained, "usually, it involves your senses. When subjects in a study took a few minutes each day to actively savor something, they usually hurried through—eating a meal, drinking a cup of tea, walking to the bus—they began experiencing more joy, happiness, and other positive emotions, with fewer depressive symptoms."

Jessica, a 51-year-old teacher and single mother of twins, is a master of savoring. Every day, she makes a point of noticing one thing that makes her grateful, something she can savor, even in the most difficult of times. Although her divorce was very painful, she was happy again after a couple of weeks out of the marriage. She told me, "I knew I could financially take care of myself, so that made me happy. I could go out and meet new single men, and that made me happy. No one was controlling my every move, and that made me happy. I love the view outside my window, having my summers free— and the women I work with are marvelous. Every day, I find something to appreciate about my life. It's fun."

Worrywarts Are Not Attractive

If you don't love yourself, you cannot love others.
—Dalai Lama

Your mom is a worrywart, her mom was a worrywart, and so you are worrywart—it just runs in the genes! Somewhere along the road, we were led to believe that if you were a worrier, you would be a better mother. Or that somehow, worrying was an authentic sign of affection. Sorry, it's a lie. Mental apprehension does not affect any situation one way or the other. I mean, honestly, have you ever made anything better by simply worrying about it? If you answered yes, I want to meet you because we can make a lot of money selling your services. If you answered no, I want to thank you for being honest. Worrying also inhibits you from being in the moment. When you can get yourself to see beyond the angst, you can get to the savor.

Melanie, a preschool assistant and 40-year-old recently single mom of two children, stopped worrying about the why of her marriage ending and found bliss in just being. She said, "I am actually very relieved to be alone, having tolerated an intolerable situation for years in the hope that everything would work out. The fact that I gave as much as I could for my marriage and family enables me to have peace with the decision to separate."

She does not feel anger towards her ex-husband anymore. "The problems we had were his problems, his inner pain, and really had nothing to do with me," she said. "I can walk away from him. He can't run from himself. This is why I feel so free and also so compassionate." Watching her two children play and laugh is what brings her the greatest joy.

Raise Your Hand If You're Here

The meeting of two eternities, the past and
future...is precisely the present moment.
—Henry David Thoreau

In order to create a future with the important people in your life, you need to inhabit the present. Counterintuitive? Not really. Being in the *right here, right now* will make you super-aware of your feelings and interactions with others. When you live consciously and in the moment, your interpersonal skills are powerfully and positively affected. I often remind my REAL One of this *right here, right now gift* by telling him how much I love what we have together at that very moment in time.

I love spending time talking with my guy. Where we are in our lives right now, with our schedules and wrangling respective teenagers, we normally only have the weekends to spend time together. We can engage in conversation for hours on end, but somewhere in the middle of a Saturday or Sunday, he'll say, "I miss you." Usually, we still have 24 more hours together, but he is already days into the future. He's thinking about how he is going to feel Tuesday when we are not with each other instead of being present with me in the moment we are currently sharing. Although I love that he'll miss me during the week, I sometimes have to remind him, "Be with me, right here…right now." And he comes back.

Mindfulness boosts your awareness of how you interpret and react to what's happening in your mind. It increases the gap between emotional impulse and action, allowing you to do what Buddhists call recognizing the spark before the flame. Instead of lashing out in anger, backing down in fear, or mindlessly indulging a passing craving, you get the opportunity to be centered within yourself and separate your feelings from your reactions. You will feel more connected to the people around you.

Go With The Flow

The most complete way of living in the moment is when you are in the state of flow. Flow happens when you are so engrossed in something that you lose track of everything else around you. Most people are able to attain this state at one point or another while doing something that they absolutely love doing. The activity is so intrinsically rewarding that although the task may be physically challenging, the action feels effortless. To get in gear with your flow, you must set the stage and create the optimal conditions for it to occur. Set a flow goal that's challenging but not unattainable—something to which you have to marshal your attention resources and stretch your focus to achieve. In *flow*, you're firing on all cylinders to rise to a challenge. One of my favorite flow spaces is exercising. Yours might be walking your dog, playing with your children at the park, or tending to your garden. If you *really* want to go all out, try to flow with your man during lovemaking.

Sue has learned over time to be in her flow zone. She said, "Thinking about the past can make me melancholy. The future is frustrating because I can't control it. I always say, 'You are where you are meant to be,' and my *right here, right now* is in my garden. I call it 'my organic Xanax.' When too much is going on in the exterior, I go to the interior. The garden is where my heart and mind come together—it's my happy place."

Be In The Bother

When I am anxious, it is because I am living in the future.
When I am depressed, it is because I am living in the past.
—Anonymous

As humans, we'd prefer to hum along happily day after day as if we were riding in the Autopia cars at Disneyland. Life doesn't work that way, and it shouldn't. The only way we can grow to be better mothers and lovers is not to avoid the bothersome situations that pop up in life but rather face them head-on. They require us to step up, take note and make an adjustment. In spiritual psychology, we term these events or people in our lives that create this turmoil "stackers." They're like messengers that show us, with terrifying clarity, exactly where we're stuck. These stackers will show up time and time again until we face the issue and deal with what's being dealt.

Dana, a 39-year-old schoolteacher and single mom of two girls, says the only solution is acceptance. That is, be open to the way things are in each moment without trying to manipulate or change the experience. Don't judge it, cling to it, or push it away. Acceptance is freeing and relieves you of needless extra suffering.

Dana has found a way to move on with no resentment toward her ex. "I got to the point that I finally understood that his infidelities were not about me—that it was not that there was something I was not giving him or lacking," she said. "I had obsessed for years on why he was doing this to me. It was all about him and wanting him to want the marriage. I finally really looked at what I wanted and realized he was not capable of giving that to me."

Once she realized that, it was as if a switch had been turned off and she was ready to move on. It took her many, many years to understand this, but now she is in a good place, being happy just with her girls.

Like Dana, if you feel anxiety, sadness, or anger about an event that has transpired in your life, accept the feelings, label them and go to your happy place. In those quiet moments, your thoughts, perceptions, and emotions will flit through your mind. You will come to understand that your thoughts are just thoughts. You don't have to believe them, and you don't have to do what they say.

Know That You Don't Know

Instead of adding days to your life, add life to your days.
—Kerri Zane

You might want to believe that if there were never any "uh-ohs" or "not agains," your days would be smooth and life could be sweet. But that blissful wonderment of knowing that you don't know everything and the curveballs in life are what make it worth living and is where you'll find joy. Be good with the unexpected in the *right here, right now* of your day. You will wake up every morning to new and fresh surprises. My girlfriend likes to call it the "pie in the sky moments." Your life can feel ho-hum and sad until you suddenly get that call, e-mail, text, or IM that spins your life around. Those are the embraceable and exciting events that make life worth living!

Forty-two year old Kathy, a lawyer and single mom of two, expressed this best about moving through her divorce into single motherhood. "One of the things I think we single moms need to acknowledge is that pining for the past 'couldas' or 'shouldas' doesn't propel us forward. I thought I was going to be grandparents with that man, but that's not the way it turned out. So I gave myself permission to mourn the future I realized I would never have. Then I unstuck myself from my divorce place, rid myself of future angst and stopped worrying about what might be. The future became an exciting place full of opportunity."

The past is history. The future is a mystery. Today is
a gift—that is why it's called the present.
—Anonymous

Part Two:

THE OUTSIDE 5

6 BALANCE YOUR MULTI-PLATFORMS

Women need real moments of solitude and self-reflection
to balance out how much of ourselves we give away.
—Barbara De Angelis

To-Dos And Not To-Dos—That Is The Question

Every single mom's life is packed with "to-dos." There isn't a moment in the day when someone or something isn't pulling you in a zillion different directions. Between school activities, team-mom duties, attending meetings, taking care of the car, keeping up with the house or apartment, shopping for food, fixing meals, reviewing homework, getting kids to bed on time, working a full-time job (some of us must), handling the ex and, if you are like me, caring for an aging parent or two, we're a busy bunch. Where does one fit in the REAL One shopping time? It is all-important, and thankfully, it can all be juggled with just a few multi-platform balancing adjustments.

Though it appears that a single mom's life is much more challenging than the married mom's, it's not necessarily so. Actually, the majority of single moms interviewed reported that once they went solo, their lives became less stressful and more streamlined, since there was no one to answer to and no one looking over their shoulder anymore.

Mary, a 42-year-old single mom of two and entrepreneur, supported this sentiment. During her marriage, Mary was a slave to her inflexible work calendar. She was the primary wage earner, so it was her responsibility to cover all of her family expenses. She missed her daughter's soccer games and taking her son to school in the morning. The unhappier she became in her marriage, the more she buried herself in her job and the less time she spent at home with her children. It was not a healthy balance. Then she made significant changes all at once. She decided to leave her marriage and simultaneously start her own business. That was a few years ago. Today, her business is growing steadily, and she's excited about the future. Mary has less income right now, but she's happier because she has more time with her children. She told me, "I haven't wanted to talk about my divorce much because I didn't want people to see me differently. Being a single mom doesn't mean you're needy or out of sorts. I function very well on my own. I am more in balance now than I ever was when I was married."

Mary found that being a single mom provided her with the ability to employ important balancing mechanisms, time-management skills and the power of the absolute "No!"

Building "N-O!" Boundaries (For One And All)

When you can't say no, you give up what's essential
to you in favor of what other people want.
—Dr. William Ury, Ph.D.

You were so good at saying "No!" when you were two! What happened? For most women it seems that the submissive, "yes behavior" is predicated on the stone-cold belief that if you say no to someone, that particular someone is not going to like you. This is because of that finely tuned people-pleaser way of being that you've so adeptly honed to perfection over the years. It's exactly what has gotten you into this pickle now. You are living up to everyone else's expectations. Yes, even your ex – but why do you do that? Who says everyone has to like you? It'll never happen. And maybe you don't like that person (your ex) who asked you to do that thing you don't want to do anyway, so why should you care if he likes you? Bottom line: Until you utter the word or express the sentiment of "No!" to him (or others), you'll never know how the receiver is going to respond.

According to Dr. William Ury in his book "The Power of a Positive No," there are several ways to get the gloriously freeing ability to utter the unequivocal "No!" The first step is to get clear on what is essential and important for you to say yes to in your life. Check in with the Living Vision you've created for yourself in Chapter 1 and determine if what the person has asked you to do fits somewhere on your page. If it's incongruous, "No!" should be the only sound spilling from your lips.

Gia, a 45-year-old single mother of two, was the consummate people pleaser until everyone else's requests became overwhelming and she became physically ill.

"Its feels good now to say no," Gia said, "but it took a lot to get me to that place." It was her choice to leave her marriage, but it manifested as a weighty load of guilt. No matter what her ex or the kids asked of her, especially when it came to the children's needs, she'd agree to do it. She didn't want anyone to be upset with her. Her ex convinced Gia that her decision to leave the marriage had hurt everyone in the family enough already. So even if his requests were incredibly unreasonable, she would force herself to get them done. Then a year after her divorce, Gia was diagnosed with breast cancer. "It hit me," she said. "The stress of overdoing everything was killing me." At that point, Gia released herself from the guilt. Saying no to her ex and occasionally her children was a fate far less dangerous than her illness. Remarkably, they managed to get everything taken care of without her. "When I stopped caring about him and stood my ground about what was important to me—getting healthy—the better I felt about myself," Gia said.

Gia found that saying no to her ex in spite of the consequences to their relationship was a resounding "Yes!" to herself. If she can do it, so can you.

"No!" Timing

Until you value your time, you will not do anything with it.
—M. Scott Peck

Ury goes on to instruct that the first and most valuable piece of the "No!" timing puzzle to get is that no matter who is making a request of you, do not respond on the spot. This way, you won't say yes under pressure or react emotionally to the request, especially when you're feeling pressured. When you allow a day or even an hour or two of physical and mental distance from the request, it allows you time for perspective. Think about whose interests are at stake, what's really being asked of you and, as mentioned above, whether it makes sense within the construct of your living vision to say yes. Once you make up your mind, particularly if your answer is going to be "No!" don't leave the person hanging indefinitely. Avoiding the "No!" response is not only impolite but it also sends the wrong message. You risk the chance that the person requesting the favor will believe that your silence is an open invitation to pander to your people-pleasing sensibility.

My mom is a master at this game. She's the Queen of Requests, and at 92 years old, she makes it nearly impossible for me to turn her down. There are weeks when the demands come fast and furious. I have to remind myself to take a moment (or even a day) before automatically answering in the affirmative. Sometimes when I don't respond immediately to her, she works through the issue and finds another solution. Other times, I will turn down her request, and though it is not the answer she wants to hear, she eventually recovers and loves me again. Of course, I'm her daughter!

Often, even when I say no, my Mom will continue with her unwavering persistence in the hope that I'll change my answer. For her and others like her, the non-confrontational "yes-no-yes" approach works well. First, share what you're currently saying yes to. ("Mom, I am taking my daughter to her music class."). Then say no. ("So I won't be able to help you clean out your closet."). But don't stop there. After you've turned someone down, affirm your good intentions by closing with another yes to a mutually positive outcome. ("But I'd be happy to come over at another time and help you."). This "gentler" method of "No!" will relieve the person's frustration coming from your turning them down and will also send the message that you respect his or her needs.

'No!' Kidding

What if your goal were to start saying yes just a little more slowly?
—Anonymous

As a single mom, it is often most difficult to say no to your children. The culpability of breaking up a family, regardless of who's done the deed, always plays a heavy role when it comes to a child's request—any request. Sheryl Kane, a single mom, educator, and parenting consultant, told me that single moms are the worst at standing their ground with children. They tell their kids something and then end the statement with "Okay?" as if it were a question that needed their approval. She advises her clients that it is time to stop asking children if it's okay with them. If they think you aren't comfortable with your decision unless they're comfortable, they will push back. At the end of the day, it is not what you want; truthfully, they don't really feel good either about pushing you into their choice. Stay firm in your commitment (choice), be aware of your behavior and retrain yourself to make a statement rather than ask a question. Stop giving away your power!

Have faith that your children are resilient. In fact, you will find that they are more resilient than you. So the "No!" you think is going to be so painful for them may just roll off their backs. Remember, kids see the world through a kid-centric periscope. In other words, YOU are their personal service provider. Most of the time, you are there for them—no question. Sometimes, though, their requests will require more of your time than is reasonable. When this happens, it is a special opportunity for you to flex your "No!" muscle and allow your child to learn the value of Mom. They get to experience you standing up for yourself even in the throes of being a devoted mom.

Faye, a project manager and 52-year-old mother of two became divorced when her children were five and seven. Travelling for her job 50 weeks out of the year left little room for bickering in her life. "I wasn't home a lot, so I had to make special the time we had," she said. Faye would employ the "*What can we do?*" attitude when it came to getting things done around the house. So for example, instead of pushing her son to clean his room and getting that stubborn no answer, she'd ask him, "What *can* you do?" If his answer was that he could clean the top of his desk that is what would get done. Making the effort was good enough for Faye and certainly better than creating a household firestorm.

Faye found a very creative way to have peaceful positive experiences with her children, turning their no's into yeses and her no's into acceptable yeses. Children are resourceful and love to be empowered.

Sometimes however the children come in larger sizes. EX-tra large that is!

'Ex-Man' Overboard!

> *And in fact, I think the challenge is not*
> *in the "No!" It's in the default "Yes."*
> **—Anonymous**

If the over-the-top request comes from your ex-hubby, do your best to avoid responding with a long burdensome story. Remember this acronym: KISS the frog goodbye, which stands for Keep It Simple, Sister. Any story you roll out to the frog, he can use to his advantage. Frankly, the more drawn out your excuse the less authentic it sounds and in the end, whatever your story is it's really no one else's business. In this case, less is more effective!

If the ex gets worked up and reactive after you've delivered your "No!" do not yield under his pressure. Take a deep breath and listen attentively but with a definitively removed ear to his objections. Then, gently but firmly explain that you understand why this is important to him and underscore your inability to accommodate his request at this time. Continue to keep your response simple and clean. Do not backpedal or become defensive. Keep your living vision in mind. It's about your time, your resources, your respect, and your goals. If all else fails and you are an incurable softie, have a Plan B already in place and be ready to follow through with it if need be.

Kendra, a 38-year-old teacher and single mom of three, was always being pulled in a dozen different directions at once. Especially after her separation, she became a serial overcommitter. Kendra would take on a committee job for every activity that each of her kids participated in. Then, inevitably, she'd end up double-booked and have someone or another upset with her when she'd show up late or not at all. At the same time, she had signed up for a dating service, but every time they had a guy for her, she was too busy to make the date. "They said they were going to fire me as a client because I was never available!" Kendra said. "Can you imagine?" Being on all the committees was helpful, but it wasn't time spent with her kids, and it was killing her chances of finding true love. She decided that setting aside time to date was a priority and a legitimate way to say no to all the other obligations. Kendra's Plan B was "I have another commitment." She didn't need to go into any detail about her commitment to finding a new beau because it was nobody's business. There can be no argument about her plan because it is honorable to stick to your commitments. End of story.

No-yes-no and Plan B are solid go-to strategies to support your living vision. That being said, if they don't feel right for you, do not despair—there are also statements like "Not now," "Let me think about it," and "Maybe I can help you find someone who can help you." Finally, there is the "I have a personal policy about ———— (fill in the blank)," or "I don't want to take on what I can't fully commit to doing well." Saying either of these puts the focus on your feeling, and no one can effectively argue with you about that.

Time For Mommy And For Me

We come into this world headfirst and go out feet first; in between, it is all a matter of balance.
—Paul Boese

In addition to building your arsenal of "No!" strategies, time management is key in becoming the most balanced single mother you can be. Unfortunately, most of you probably find it difficult to prioritize all the to-dos on the list; thus, the me-time activities end up way down at the bottom, or worse, they don't even make the cut. You end up feeling like a whirling dervish you don't recognize.

There are some days when I will move from one room to the next in my house picking up whatever project happens to be in front of me in that spot and doing a little bit. Then I remember that I didn't finish the first project I started and go back to that one. I can go a whole day never completing anything. To heal this affliction, I have to take a deep breath and say to myself, "Okay, go back and finish what you started before you move on to the next." I look like a crazy woman, my children think I'm nuts, but it helps! I am a huge fan of the daily to-do lists. I make my list reasonable; in other words, I only put on the daily list what I know I can accomplish in that one day. I write my lists on little sticky notes so they can't be too long. Then, when the list is completed, I have the gratification of tossing the sticky in the trash.

Additionally, you might find it helpful to create monthly to-do lists. Spend a half-hour or so at the beginning of every month and brainstorm all the necessary things you think you would like to accomplish. Then, give each a priority number of 1 through 10. Make 1 the most important and 10 the least important. If you are anything like the nearly 85 percent of single moms I spoke with, you're making the majority of your to-dos about either work or helping your kids. Thus, instead of making me-time activities, like finding your REAL One, a low priority (i.e., higher number). I suggest you try putting "dating" once a week a me-time 5 or lower number on your to-do list.

Helping Hands

Time is what we want most, but what we use worst.
—William Penn

Many single moms, or about-to-be single moms, think they need to have 100 percent of the lion's-share custody of their kids in order to continue to receive their Good Mother Gold Star. Unfortunately, there are no guarantees on either account. That means it's time to delegate and work on a custody arrangement that suits all aspects of your life, not just the mommy part. So, unless your ex-spouse is physically or emotionally abusive or unfit to be a parent because of drugs or alcohol, go for a more evenly distributed child-custody arrangement. Studies show this is best for kids. Plus, your noncustodial time is the perfect opportunity to schedule personal downtime and dating escapades.

I had a 50/50 split with my former husband—one week on and one week off. At first, I hated the arrangement and cried every Monday when my children went back to their dad for his seven-day share. A year into this arrangement, I got used to the idea. I really began to enjoy my bifurcated mommy time and me time. On the off weeks, I hung out with friends, charged through work projects, or focused on meeting new men. It was the perfect time to search online without little child eyes spying over my shoulder.

If you cannot negotiate a fair child-custody arrangement with your children's daddy or choose not to take that route, there are other ways to find time for yourself. Don't get into the mindset that you are the only one who can do the job. Feel comfortable asking for help. Releasing responsibility to others alleviates that single mom "need" to be superhuman and allows for a huge sigh of relief. Enlist family and friends to help or offer tag-team time-sharing with other single moms.

You are entitled to have some adult "me time." Don't let anyone or anything distract you from taking the time to enjoy your life. Without rest and relaxation, you cannot be the most magnificent you!

> *Time is a created thing. To say "I don't*
> *have time" is to say "I don't want to."*
> **—Lao Tzu**

7 RETROFITTING YOUR FINANCIALS

Back In The Game

I'm living so far beyond my income that
we may almost be said to be living apart.
— e.e. Cummings

I was in a Pilates class recently with four other women, three of them married. The fourth had just lost her husband to a dirty one-bedroom apartment and a much younger blonde. The other ladies were consoling the new singleton, assuring her that "don't worry— he'll pay!" Not necessarily, I interjected. After a round of horrified glances from the group, the married ringleader retorted, "Well, the courts make ex-husbands pay alimony and child support! She's going to be fine."

Boy, did *she* need a wake-up call, and so do a lot of women. Many mothers think the same thing when they contemplate divorce. But when you bite the bullet and serve the papers, or get them served to you, living high off your old hog is not necessarily the rule—it's rather the exception. If you were one of the ladies who opted for the club brunch rather than the power lunch, you are in for a rude awakening. Everything you thought or imagined to be your financial safety net is gone. The ties have been severed, and you are in free fall.

No one has learned this difficult lesson more than Kaitlin, an immigrant to this country. She was only 25 years old and barely able to speak English when the man she would later marry swept her off her feet in only six months. Now, this 41-year-old quintessentially perfect stay-at-home wife and mom is in the midst of a horrific separation.

She told me, "Every year that passed in my 16-year marriage felt like another year that my husband swallowed whole pieces of me." She worked tirelessly, doing whatever it took to keep her family together and her husband's business successful. But it was never enough for him. He would lash out at her with unexpected tirades. She recalled, "He'd be reading the Bible and calling me names all at the same time. It was like he was trying to 'break' me." Kaitlin survived his criticisms by becoming numb. Then she realized she wasn't really living anymore— she was just functioning. It took everything she had to walk away from that marriage—more strength than she knew she possessed. He was furious.

In the throes of her nasty divorce battle, her ex-husband has cut off every penny of support for her and the children. Kaitlin says she wakes up in the middle of the night in a cold sweat thinking that she and her children might be living out on the streets. Although having to find a job at her age wasn't how she expected her life to turn out, Kaitlin has no other choice. Nevertheless, she remains optimistic because she feels like herself again.

Kaitlin and her husband have plenty of company. Each year, there are nearly one million couples in the United States who are torturing each other while dividing assets and time-sharing children. It is a sad commentary on our choices and level of commitment to the marriage contract, but the real tragedy lies in the financial devastation heaped on so many mothers and their children. One in five married men in this country has a secret bank account or credit card he keeps from his other half. Eighty percent have admitted to lying to their spouse about their overspending. If a woman's desire is to readily kick her career to the curb while opting to be a homemaker, she's living with her financial head in the sand, and that will prove to be her ultimate demise.

The ugly truth is this: Divorce makes a father potentially richer and, in the worst-case scenario, can send a woman into poverty. Recent statistics show that the average man experiences a 15 percent improvement in his standard of living following divorce. In comparison, his ex-spouse will suffer a 45 percent loss in her standard of living. By staying consistently employed, men continue to advance their careers and employment status, thus increasing earnings and perpetuating their financial potential. It also allows them easier access to hiding personal assets. So, while the chance to be a stay-at-home mom sounds like early-retirement nirvana, the reality is that the longer you're out of the workforce, the harder it can be to jump back in. You lose out on all the advantages your mate is afforded. As divorce looms large, former stay-at-home moms face a long gap in employment history, which translates to lowball wage offers and lesser job titles than you could have expected had you not opted out of the real world for diaper duties.

Unlike Kaitlin, Laura, a lawyer and 42-year-old single mom of two teenage daughters, was a working mom from the get-go and had an entirely different divorce experience. Laura was in the middle of law school when she met her husband and, in spite of her husband's objections, was insistent on completing her education. When her children were young, she worked part-time. Four years before her husband moved out, she went back full-time. "It was a godsend, because when we filed for divorce, there was no arguing over the usual alimony issues," Laura told me. "I'm not saying divorce is easy—it's not. The fact that I knew I could support my children and myself without their father's help allowed me to sleep at night."

Of course, hindsight is 20/20, but if you are contemplating a divorce and not currently working like Kaitlin, it's time to get back in the employment game. If you are employed, stay put.

Only Lawyers Win

If you've already completed your divorce, you may want to skip ahead to **Money: Moving Forward** for some solid tips on single-mom financial management. If you haven't started your proceedings or you are just at the beginning of your process, I suggest you explore all your options before lawyering up. Having the high-powered super-expensive attorney does not guarantee that you will effortlessly boot the extra boy baggage, snag a hefty child-support check, and settle your community assets with a substantial alimony payment to solidify your comfortable retirement. Nobody wins financially in divorce except the lawyers!

The green bleeding starts the moment you meet your lawyer. First, there's a significant retainer fee and the unparalleled ability of the majority of divorce lawyers to add fuel to your emotional flames. The more you and your soon-to-be ex-husband fight, the more hours the lawyers work and the more money they make. You will be surprised by how they can ensure that you'll argue over innumerable issues that will require them to send letters and documents flying back and forth between legal offices. Each letter, 15-minute phone call, e-mail, fax, and copied document costs you money. Some lawyers' even bill for the time spent billing!

There are lots of issues to consider in dividing financial assets— enough to fill another book, in fact. Suffice it to say that the bottom line is that the legal system is messy. Even women who "won" their divorce with legal representation paid too high a price for it, financially and emotionally. Rather than bicker, the key for you and your former husband is to retain your hard-earned assets. If you can both keep your focus on what is in the best interest of your new independent households and your children instead of getting even with each other, you will all come out better. And the cleanest way to accomplish this is to not go to war in the first place!

Masterful Mediation

It is pretty hard to tell what does bring happiness;
poverty and wealth have both failed.
—Kin Hubbard

Marriage is a contract. That contract is the legally binding certificate you receive when you go to the county courthouse and get married. This contractual aspect of the man/woman union predates recorded history. Back in the day, before we took finding a mate into our own hands and chose to unite in "love," marriages were arranged for the financial gain of each respective family. For better or worse, marriage was and is a business arrangement. In spite of what you are feeling, the action of uniting as husband and wife is commerce. So it stands to reason in divorce that the dissolution of your marriage is also just business.

When you can put your fury aside and become a rational human being, you can leave the courtrooms behind and peacefully work out a mutually beneficial mediation. Mediation isn't about winning or losing—it's about fairly settling your affairs in a fashion so that harmony can prevail as you and your ex move forward with your newly defined nuclear family. Professional mediators are trained to not "take sides." Rather, it is their job to work out a settlement that is fair and equitable for both parties. They are equipped to handle financial issues like division of assets, child support, child maintenance, and child custody. They can even assist in arranging the custody of a pet. This way of dealing with divorce is far less expensive and time-consuming than traditional litigation. The less money you spend quarreling over money is cash you can use to support your lifestyle and care for your children. The mediation process can take a third or less of the time of a full-on legal battle, and there is only one person's fees to pay for both of you. Before signing on the dotted line, you can hire independent counsel to reassure yourself that the arrangement is equitable.

Of course, when you choose mediation, you also have to be realistic in your outcome expectations. Mediators are not miracle workers. Divorcing will absolutely affect your lifestyle. It just makes rational sense that two people who each maintain independent households can't exist as cheaply as two people living as a single unit.

Melinda, a 40-year-old entrepreneur and single mom of two, smartly chose to mediate. "I saw how much my friends spent on their divorces, even down to their last $80. And the more bitter and angry they became, the worse it got," she said. Melinda is correct— more than the money, one of the hardest parts of divorces is how it psychologically affects the children. Melinda did not want her kids to become pawns. She and her former husband were able to check their egos at the door and proceed with a very amicable mediation. Neither pays the other child support or alimony. The kids are a shared responsibility, so they split the expenses evenly. "He's a good dad, and the kids love him," Melinda said. "We agreed our relationship was over and there was no reason to make the process any more challenging."

One final bit of advice should you choose to drop the lawyers is to make certain the mediator you choose is specifically trained in tax issues related to divorce and to the laws of the state in which you are divorcing.

Can You Collaborate?

In the collaborative divorce process, each party has his or her own attorney who is certified in mediation and collaborative law. You and your former spouse can be in that enviable place of authentically preserving an amicable relationship and doing what is best for everyone involved over the long term. Andrea Vacca,

P.C., a certified mediator and collaborative lawyer, explained that in collaboration, lawyers are focused on the best interest for all parties concerned, including the children, versus each party's position in the divorce chess game. All parties sign a "participation agreement" with each client. Each lawyer agrees that he or she will make best efforts to resolve all the conflicts without going to court and using no adversarial strategies or litigation. It is all done with respect and complete transparency; therefore, all communications during the process are conducted at the bargaining table. No one takes advantage of errors made by the other party.

The collaborative divorce is a team approach in that each former spouse is supported throughout the process by using a host of professionals, each of whom is an expert in his or her field of practice. In other words, there is a certified divorce coach to help with the emotional button-pushing triggers, a financial planner, an estate-planning attorney, an accountant, and/or a certified divorce financial analyst. You may also want to retain a therapist, a career counselor, or a qualified domestic-relations order (QDRO) specialist (for pension or retirement account divisions). QDRO pros are trained in highly technical issues such as how to split a retirement account or how to split a family business in a way that allows it to stay intact.

Stephanie, a yoga instructor, freelance writer, and 43-year-old single mom of one son, felt that just because she and her husband could not be married anymore did not mean that either she or her ex was interested in creating a war zone for their son to have to navigate through.

What Stephanie liked best about the collaborative process is that her son never became a pawn in the proceedings. "When the child-custody issues—like which pediatrician to use or who would pay for class trips and holiday schedules—became an issue, the lawyers suggested we bring in a family therapist," she said. "Our lawyers explained that we were then paying one person, rather than the two lawyers, to resolve an issue where the therapist had the expertise. I don't know how any parent can go to court and argue with a former spouse and then come home and be present for their child. I'm glad it never got ugly. Don't get me wrong—there are times when I don't like my ex, but we are not at war."

Money: Moving Forward

The mint makes it first; it is up to you to make it last.
—Evan Esar

Congratulations! If you've gotten to this point and lived to talk about it, you have undoubtedly faced the largest single financial and legal transaction of your life. No matter how it all turned out, the next steps are critical for the balance of your future. Assuming your big-ticket expenses as they relate to your children—orthodontics and college, for instance—have been handled through your divorce proceedings, it's now time to focus on your needs. Where are you going to live? Will you buy or rent? What is your new lifestyle going to be? How much will it cost you to support yourself and your offspring? How will you generate income? If you are receiving spousal support, how will it be received, and for how long? If you received a lump sum, how will you invest it? Making the right decisions can go a long way toward ensuring that you have a comfortable retirement and provide adequately for your kids—and even your grandkids.

Take the time to meet with your financial advisor to help steer you in the right direction in terms of what you can afford for your living situation. Together, you will determine your earning potential and practical retirement scenarios. Assuming you are fortunate enough to have a portfolio, you will decide how aggressively you should invest. In other words, how much of *your* money (don't you like the sound of that!) is invested in stocks, how much to put into bonds, and how much should remain in cash.

In addition to how you settle your basic living costs and investments, you need to be uber-smart this time around in the big-picture scheme of finding your new man and how you share your financial package.

Helen Georgaklis, a 44-year-old single mom of two, knows more than anyone what it is to be an at-risk single mom, having been a woman on the edge several times over. After the second man in her life left her with no resources, she was able to muster her extraordinary smarts to not only survive but also thrive. Now, with 10-plus years as a financial planner and the founder and publisher of the 99 Book Series of self-help books, she shares this advice with all of her single-mom sisters.

"The minute you have signed those papers, you get a clean piece of paper and write the top three financial issues you *have* to tackle," Ms. Georgaklis lays them out as follows:

1. Always put half of every dollar you earn, even if it's only a dollar, in your savings account. You MUST not have access to it and you MUST remain as disciplined as possible. Yes, there may be times when you cannot always put half, but still, put something away. In a year, you can actually have a couple thousand dollars saved.

2. "Retail therapy" has its merits, but it has to be tempered. The best feeling in the world is looking good, especially when you are emotionally not "looking so good," however at the end of the day shopping is a temporary fix. Do not let emotions run your money! It never ends well and shopping is usually the first "venting" you do. The key is to look good ALL the way past retirement, not just today.

3. Now is not the time to share. While you were married, you shared your finances, thoughts, feelings, beds and bathrooms! You must never share your money with anyone again. If it's one thing I tell women all the time, you deserve to be pampered, so stop feeling like you have to give it back. Yes, show them how you feel, but keep money out of it. Let your money be your best-kept secret!

Money is intertwined with every aspect of your life—your home, your children's education, even the quality of your care. As Helen's instructed, be smart with the cash you've got—it will give you a sense of peace. A word to the wise: As the newly empowered romantic businesswoman, should you decide to remarry, a prenuptial agreement is absolutely justifiable. It doesn't mean you love him any less or that either one of you is predetermining the demise of your new union. It's just a lot easier to negotiate the terms of a divorce on the front end rather than at the back, just to be secure. You will not be alone—a portion of matrimonial lawyers surveyed reported that there is a significant increase in prenups and that 52 percent of the requests are coming from women.

Ultimately, the goal is for you to hang on to what you've got. After all, you are not getting any younger.

I don't like money, actually, but it quiets my nerves.
—**Joe Louis**

8 LOVE YOUR VESSEL

There is only one temple in the world and that is the
human body. Nothing is more sacred than that noble form.
—Novalis

As a mother, I believe we are conditioned to self-sacrifice. It's a wobbly tightrope walk of balancing Mom's needs and child's needs. Then there are all the other forces that pull at you, including—and especially—former spouses. Add to that the childcentric inconveniences caused as a result of your split; the added household responsibilities loaded onto your plate and a heaping dose of divorce guilt can result in a lack of me-time self-care. Contrary to what you've rationalized, applying self-love by cherishing your vessel and taking time to honor your body by exercising to stay fit is the most unselfish gift you can give to yourself and everyone around you. Not only is it necessary for optimum health but also you garner outer body confidence, and that is what will draw your REAL One in. The inner confidence you exude as a result will entice him to want to get to know you better.

Diane, a once full-figured beauty and now a 54-year-old single mom of two, learned this lesson the hard way. Diane was living with her fiancé, the love of her life, when her mother became seriously ill. The responsibility of caring for her mom took a toll, and Diane started to gain weight. "After a while, my clothes didn't fit anymore," she said. "I had to wear an Oprah Winfrey Bucket Bra, and I ballooned to over 200 pounds. I was miserable." Her guy was sweet—he never said anything. "But when we made love, I would see my boobs hanging down, my stomach dragging on the ground—and I'd hear the unpleasant sounds of two heavy people in the act. It disgusted me," she said. "I would think to myself, how could he even want to touch me? After a while, my sex drive died, and then I lost him."

Diane's body image and self-esteem had hit rock bottom. Ultimately, it was her lack of self-confidence that sent her guy packing. Surprisingly, women don't have to tip the scale at 200 to lack confidence.

Body Image Rewire

Lack of activity destroys the good condition of every human being, while movement and methodical physical exercise save it and preserve it.
—Plato

A recent survey asked a number of females if they felt it was possible for plus-size women to have self-esteem. The collective response was mainly positive. When asked if they themselves would have self-confidence if they were overweight, they unequivocally responded no. In other words, women believe in theory that they should not equate self-worth with size, but in reality, they still do. Nearly three-quarters of the women interviewed said they wished they could wear a smaller size, even the ones who were already a slim size 8. And this is not something you can just fix with a serious sit-down self-talk. The penchant to be "body dimorphic," or having an image of your physical self that is different from how it actually appears, is in our genes.

Anthropologic scientists claim that women more than men are hardwired to put more emphasis on looks. The value of attractiveness has been programmed into women's DNA as a survival encoding. Perceived physical beauty was necessary to help a woman snag a mate and ultimately to ensure that the union would stay intact. It worked for cavewomen. Fast-forward a few thousand years and it's obvious that this "pretty principle" is still in play for ladies today. Whether you are a woman on a subway looking for a seat or a little girl in a baby stroller, the more attractive you appear, the better treatment you receive. Think about it: Little boys and men are valued for their strength and intelligence, while women and girls are doted on for their looks. This kind of thinking has become inscribed into our brains.

As a result, we have become the masters of critically measuring our own attractiveness. Self-denigration is the most damaging thought pattern a woman can inflict on her self-esteem because it is so personal. And women don't just denigrate themselves privately—it's also a group sport. When a woman critiques herself in front of her friends, she is projecting onto them as well. Add a dose of ugly divorce dialogue from a former spouse, and your self-esteem is at an all-time low.

Getting Physical

How beautiful it is to express yourself through your body and exercise. How thrilling to experience energy at such a level.
—Steve Chandler

It takes a strong woman and a concerted effort to combat the hellfire mix of nature and nurture to regain a healthy inside-and-outside body image. Daily exercise to become fit is a self-esteem essential. Here is the simple fact: The more in shape you become, the better you will feel about you. When your self-esteem gets a boost, you care more about yourself. Then, doing things that are good for you, like eating a healthier diet and exercising regularly, become your daily de rigueur. You will innately be more diligent about your training. It's a 360-degree cycle of self-fulfilling happiness and the unbroken bond between your inner and outer selves, which equates to that awe inspiring total self-confidence.

Several years back, at 23 years old, Ellen, an office manager, found herself to be a single mom of three young children ages five and younger. Her salve for the pain and suffering of divorce was smoking. She was on a runaway train toward the Grim Reaper. Through a magical mix of exercising and meditation, she came to understand that she was meant to be happy, healthy and in control rather than ravaging her body with bad behavior.

"As a single mom of three children—five, three, and one—I combined affirmations like 'I can' and 'I am good enough' and 'I release fear' with exercises to help me feel competent and confident," she said. After her divorce, working out with the affirmations was instrumental in helping her feel good about herself. If you don't like yourself, it's hard to find others who do. "Dating was important, yet I was learning to love myself, and so outside confirmations of my worth and value as a woman were secondary to my own need for self-care," Ellen said. Her technique of combining the affirmations with movements helped her create the positive changes that she wanted in her life.

The Well-Maintained Winners

A (wo)man's health can be judged by which
she takes two at a time—pills or stairs.
—Joan Welsh

When should you start your exercise program? Uhhhh…now! In the book *The Healing Power of Exercise: Your Guide to Prevention and Treating Diabetes, Depression, Heart Disease, High Blood Pressure, Arthritis, and more,* authors Dr. Linn Goldberg and Diane Elliot state, "A universal finding in exercise studies is that people experience a greater sense of well-being." The improvement in mood begins just 10 minutes after the start of exercising, and the sunny-side-up mood continues to climb for up to 20 minutes following a workout. Follow-up studies indicated that with continuous daily workouts, the improvement in mood lasts for months. In fact, study participants who simply walked daily for seven weeks found that the enhancement in vigor continued after five months. When the participants continued to exercise, the endorphin blast and resulting happiness high were even greater. It is ongoing bliss!

Melody, a public relations entrepreneur and 36-year-old single mom to one young son, knows all about the exhilaration of exercise and how it bolsters her self-esteem.

"I am a single mom and a fitness fanatic," she told me. Her workout routine includes exercising with a mobile trainer twice a week balanced with at-home workouts. "I feel great about myself and my body," she said. "And when you are confident, it makes meeting new people and dating easier." Melody struggled with her weight for years, but now says she feels great. She advises that other single moms get into a workout that is the most convenient and easiest for them to do, because being a single mom is tough and it is hard to find extra time in the day. It's got to flow in the schedule.

The reason exercise is so critical to your overall happiness is because it regulates the stress hormone in your brain: *cortisol.* Cortisol promotes the release of endorphins. Endorphins are organic substances that occur in the neural activity of your brain. They're like nature's morphine. Working out also stimulates another chemical transmitter in your brain called *serotonin,* which is your internal happy signal, or "nature's upper!"

One of the main reasons people who exercise are more at peace with themselves is because they find that physical training, as opposed to the alternative of popping pills, gives them a personal sense of accomplishment. The conclusion of a recent study on women and exercise was that working out yields better self-confidence and more long-term self-esteem benefits than any over-the-counter mood-altering drug. You've got all the natural happy chemicals you need already installed.

Those single moms who are dedicated workout queens know the mental exhilaration of a healthy training session and derive the confidence of a successful workout. Sheryl, a 45-year old stay-at-home single mom of one daughter, is an avid cyclist. Sheryl rides her bike about 50 to 70 miles a week and goes to the gym. She has even competed in century rides during the last 10 years. Riding is really important to her, so she'll do her daily training while her daughter is sleeping in the morning or after she drops her off at school. "If I don't have time to do a ride, I definitely make sure I get to the gym," she told me. "Otherwise, I'm anxious and uneasy for the rest of the day."

Sheryl is not kidding. The day we did our interview, we started off on a bike ride, but one of her tires blew, so we had to cut the ride short. While we were talking, she was mentally calculating how long it would take us to finish our Q&A, get to the bike store to fix her tire, eat lunch, and be back out on the path to finish her training before she had to pick her daughter up from school. The girl is committed! I give her props for that.

The Time Is Now

There is no easy way out. If there were, I would have bought it.
And believe me, it would be one of my favorite things!
—Oprah Winfrey

The number-one excuse women claim for not exercising is lack of time. I understand that children are demanding and work gets in the way, not to mention all the other stuff you have to attend to as a single (working) mom. But I'd like to emphasize that you don't have the luxury to not "fit" fitness into your daily agenda. Fortunately, you don't necessarily have to go to the gym or try to find a dedicated 30 minutes of workout time because many of your everyday activities can be considered exercise. Even 10 minutes here or there throughout your day adds up! So, for example, try walking up the stairs to your office instead of taking the elevator, or park in the space farthest from the store entrance and walk the distance. Buy a pedometer and wear it all day long—you will be surprised how close you get to the surgeon general's recommended 10,000 steps a day just by simply changing simple habits as you go about your daily routines.

Most importantly, in order to stay in the dating game and attract your REAL One into your universe, you've got to be in tip-top shape. Many super disciplined moms will find the time to do what makes them feel healthy and beautiful.

Jordan, a spa director and 48-year-old mother of two, is an avid exerciser and knows just how important a svelte exterior plays in the dating game the second time around.

"I'm a single mom and very committed to fitness as well," she told me. Her strategy is to get up early and work out before her kids are up. This allows her to keep on schedule, no matter what life throws her way. She said, "It seems like we moms own the early morning, but the day is usually completely out of control by mid-afternoon!"

She tells me that she is in very good shape and looks much younger than her age. "There's no question being in good shape helps with the dating scene—not to say men are superficial, but they definitely seem to have something for slim women," she said. "I'm 48 years old, weigh 120 pounds, am a size 3, and eat three healthy meals a day as well as snacks." Jordan encourages other single moms to get involved. Her routine is not extreme— anyone can do it. "It just takes a little discipline to get up early," she said.

In Lori Gottlieb's book *Marry Him: The Case for Settling for Mr. Good Enough*, her dating coach, Evan, tells her, "It doesn't matter who you're looking for if he's not looking for you." So true. If a man is not attracted to you, there is nothing you can do to cajole him into feeling different. And despite the old adage that there is someone out there for everyone, a survey of males worldwide indicated that, given their druthers, they will choose a well-toned, fit woman over a too-heavy or too-thin one any day. This is programmed into their DNA, as biology dictates that a well-proportioned woman is a sign of good health and fertility. So Jordan has it right. She's doing everything she can to make herself attractive to the largest pool of desirable men for optimal REAL One choosing power.

Karen, a 47-year-old single mom of three and radio-show host, has an interesting self-rating system she uses to keep her mental and physical appearances on track.

"I have always felt that it was important to love yourself," Karen said. "Exercise is a great expression of that. It's a way to be productive and build self-confidence. Just do whatever you can to be the best you can be. That way, you radiate into a new relationship. On my radio show, *Love-Encore*, I talk about my personal and physical 1-through-10 self-rating system I've developed. If you come up short, you gotta think…what kinda guy is going to want to be with a 3 or a 4? Be confident. Do the best you can with what you got."

Fit Forever = True Love

> *You can take no credit for beauty at sixteen. But if you are beautiful at sixty, it will be your soul's own doing.*
> —**Marie Stopes**

The world of politically correct pundits might tell you that you should embrace your muffin top and saddlebags as the war wounds of parenting and aging, but science, genetics, and men are shouting a resounding "Not so much!" His ego is tied up in the woman he sashays alongside into a room. Old-school cliché dictates that you are losing out to the "younger woman." The truth is, you've got the competitive edge IF your inside matches your outside. In fact, you are poised to win. You have a clear advantage because YOU are more interesting and worldly than they are. Once you've snagged your REAL One, you're going to want to keep him, and that means a lifetime commitment to fitness. Many of the men I interviewed told me that a fit beauty will grab their attention and her confidence seals the deal. One man confided, "Men have to be attracted to the woman they are with. A strong physical attraction is critical to the level of fidelity maintained."

There is no reason why you can't be the woman they adore. Be the best physically fit woman you can be plus the charming, warm, interesting, and smart lady you've cultivated over your years on this planet. Be it all!

Leanna, an office manager and 49-year-old single mom of five, wasn't intending to take up the seven-days-a-week, 60-minutes-a-day of exercise lifestyle—it just sort of crept up on her. Now, she's an endorphin junkie!

"In March, I used my tax refund to purchase a bicycle to cut down on my monthly automobile gas bill," Leanna said. "I hadn't been on a bike for 30 years. Now, I bike into work in the morning and back home in the evening—each way is approximately a 12-mile ride. I didn't start out riding to become fit or for the exercise—I started out simply to save money. The wonderful side effects of this project have been weight loss— down from size 14 to size 8 on my way to size 6—better health and eating habits, greater self-esteem, and personal confidence. Hey! I look pretty good! I ride nearly seven days out of every week now and have a cycle coach—a friend—to help me improve my technique and stamina. At this point, I have logged in over 1,100 miles on the bike. Yes, I've become a fanatic!"

Taking care of your body through daily exercise will improve your mood and boost your self-esteem. The real lifelong gain is the resulting positive self-image, which plays a vital role in enhancing every other area of your life, especially in choosing a future relationship. In order to be willing to even engage in a new long-term REALationship, you must be confident enough to focus on what your individual needs are and be emotionally wholly centered to understand them. Again, the research is clear: when you finally begin to date, it is your self-esteem, more than any other personality trait, that will determine whether you choose to pursue a long-term relationship and with whom. When you believe that you are worthy of a great relationship with a person who has your best interest at heart, that is when you will find your REAL One.

Negatives become positives when they result in transformations.
This is how you grow, you learn and you change.
—Anonymous

9 PUT YOUR GAME FACE ON

I live and work in this world where the brain forms
a judgment on who I am in less than three seconds.
—Marcia Reynolds

It's no secret that we live on a planet that is ruled by beautiful faces. Particularly for women, being attractive is the currency that affords you respect, legitimacy, and power. It's called the "beauty premium"—in other words, a woman who takes care of herself and has an attractive appearance is open to a world of infinite options. Carefully coifed souls will find better jobs and earn more money—nearly 12 percent more—than their plain-Jane peers. People automatically assume that physical beauty implies lots of good qualities, like kindness and courtesy. This phenomenon is called the *halo effect*. No doubt, it pays to take the time and make the effort to care for your visage.

Bonnie, a former model and 57-year-old single mom of three, talked about the bennies of her beauty premium.

Bonnie's mother had been a fashion designer in Miami in the late '40s and early '50s. "She was movie-star beautiful," Bonnie said. Luckily, she inherited her mom's looks. After Bonnie's modeling career wound down, she went into business. She said that having a Southern accent and proper manners made her all the more alluring. She would use all her beauty and skills to her advantage and lower the boom at the right time. "It worked every time," she said. After many successful years in sales and marketing for several major fashion companies, Bonnie decided to start her own business. She always takes the time to keep herself fit, healthy, and attractive because she's learned that no matter what your age, being beautiful pays off.

This predisposition to be drawn to beauty is not because people are shallow. It didn't just happen overnight nor is it a result of the media's barrage of beautiful images. Though there is no doubt that the media do perpetuate an idealized vision of beauty, they are not the driving force. The truth is that the public is thirsty for appealing visions. Moviemakers, TV producers and magazine editors are delivering exactly what John Q wants. It sells. Dr. Gordon Patzer, Dean of the College of Business Administration at Roosevelt University, has spent 30 years studying and writing about physical attractiveness. He says that the eye toward beauty is anthropologically driven and has been ingrained in our DNA since the dawn of time.

Patzer postulates that humans are hardwired to respond more favorably to attractive people. Studies with babies in hospital nurseries support his hypothesis, as nurses will give special treatment to the infants who are more physically attractive, aka "cute." They will touch them more, hold them longer, and speak to them more frequently. Conversely, infants will look at attractive faces longer and more intently. This eye for beauty trend continues into grade school and beyond. When teachers interact with children of higher physical attractiveness, they will ask them more questions and prompt them for answers. The mere anticipation that these attractive children will do better propels them to fulfill the expectation. And frankly, pretty pupils will do better out in the world after their school days are done.

So, despite the pundits' backlash with books like Deborah L. Rhode's *The Beauty Bias,* the proclivity for humankind to be drawn to and enamored with an appealing face is innate. This renders the groundswell movement to implement a "beauty discrimination law" moot.

Beauty And The Streets

What does this mean to you as a single mom? A lot! Everyone whose path you cross is constantly judging you for your physical appearance. Dr. Patzer found that physicians spend more time answering questions of nice-looking female patients. Retailers will be more solicitous to attractive patrons. A well-dressed good-looking lady is eight times more likely to get street directions than someone less attractive and disheveled. In fact, not only will you get directions but also, in some cases, your "hero" will actually walk you to your destination. All of this is to say that when it comes to relationship seeking, putting your best face forward is of monumental importance.

Internet dating sites, with their vast pool of choices, have exponentially complicated the odds of meeting and capturing your REAL One's attention. Women from all over the planet are readily available right at his fingertips. This plethora of options makes the dating scene far more competitive. Online dating services will tell you that those members who post a picture get significantly more play. Furthermore, an attractive picture will get five times as many hits as a less-than-pretty counterpart. Even the dating sites will use the better-looking members as bait for recruitment. For better or worse, in order to win in today's love game, your appearance has to measure up!

Leah, an executive and 33-year-old single mom of one, is an avid online dater. Through trial and error, she learned the hard way about the do's and don'ts of presenting herself to the universe of Internet guys.

When Leah first went on a dating site a few months after her separation, she took a couple of snaps and loaded those onto her profile. The responses were less than what she'd hoped for. Then she hired a dating coach, who encouraged her to do some work on herself in order to reload her website love life. "I started working out three days a week, got regular manicures and pedicures, tried brow threading and eyelash extensions, and had the stray hairs on my upper lip removed," Leah said. "Oh, and I went to the dentist. OUCH! I looked better than I did in college!" With all that taken care of, she took some new professional shots and put them on her profile. "Now, I'm in the dating driver's seat, and I like it. I'm the one picking and choosing the good-looking guys!"

Rescripting Your Beauty Résumé

Plain women know more about men than beautiful ones do. But beautiful women don't need to know about men. It's the men who have to know about beautiful women.
—Katharine Hepburn

Surviving a divorce or death of a spouse can be emotionally difficult, and in some cases, devastating. The fact that you are a few years older, possibly still carrying "baby weight," and working on extricating your mind from any negative memories of your prior relationship can sack your beauty regimen. The mirror becomes your enemy, revealing the dark circles under your eyes and deep creases that line your face. Grey hairs seem to have popped up in unexpected places, and your teeth aren't as pearly white as they looked in your wedding photo. All this is a sucker punch to your self-esteem.

Ten years ago, Carole Brody Fleet was a 42-year-old mother of one when her then-husband fell ill and passed on. She did that typical thing widows do when they lose their lovers—she stopped caring about her outside package. Now, as the author of *Widows Wear Stilettos* and a seasoned grieving expert, she has this to say:

"When you lose someone that you loved, there is tremendous guilt. You think that you shouldn't feel good or try to look good for anyone else, because that would be disrespectful to the husband who is gone. But we all have to move on. Several months after my husband, Mike, had died, my daughter asked me when I was going to change my clothes. I realized I'd been living in my sweats and no makeup that whole time. We went to my closet together and I put on some jeans and a top. I applied a little bit of foundation to my face. I know that the introspection and inner healing takes time, and even though it wasn't a drastic makeover, it was immediate, and it made me feel better about myself. The best part was that the self-confidence I gained from being proactive about my looks made me feel like I was gaining back the control of my life that I'd thought was gone with the loss of my husband."

When you can look at yourself in the mirror and see a beautiful image reflected back, you are on your way to winning your personal battle with self-confidence. In the book *Face It*, authors Dr. Vivian Diller and Dr. Jill Muir-Sukenick, former models who counsel other models in their practice, found that a woman with ideal physical beauty who doesn't see herself as such will have low self-esteem. She will not outwardly shine as appealingly as a less-than-perfectly packaged lady who makes the most of herself and exudes her inner beauty outwardly.

So, it is up to you to decide how you want to best deal with the beauty cards in your current deck and how to manage your current mental imagery for the better. Frequently rescripting your outer-beauty résumé is the fix you need to bring the inner confidence frontward. You have a solid opportunity to live the life you want and find the REALationship you deserve.

Who's In Your Head? Get Them Out!

> *Whether a woman is visually appealing but*
> *doesn't experience herself to be, or is less attractive*
> *and does, lies in the makings of her self-image.*
> —Dr. Vivian Diller and Dr. Jill Muir-Sukenick

First and foremost, identify how you feel about your existing look and what improvements you feel you need. Dig deep and find what in your past is keeping you from working on fixing what you see as your imperfections. Whose voice is running in your head, affecting your self-image? Often, when you really listen, you will find it belongs to a person you believed had your best interest in mind. If, for example, you've been accustomed to seeing your image through the critical eye of your ex, then his negative messaging will stay with you. Or perhaps your mom denied you your unconditional beauty, leaving your positive self-esteem in disrepair. Take your time with this process and be gentle with yourself—once you can identify where the negative noise is coming from, you can manage it.

At age 44, Jacqueline P. Piper, an image enhancer and single mother, supports her clients with this philosophy: "Unhappiness is the cause of wrinkles and gray hair. It is the natural response to living away from your center. Everyone at some point must deal with this reality and begin the process of an inner-self search to discover their true-self, thus striking a happy balance in their life. The natural response to this will externalize as a beautiful human being inside and out."

That Old Devil: Fear

If you hear a voice within you say "You cannot paint,"
then by all means paint, and that voice will be silenced.
—Vincent Van Gogh

Often, what is keeping you from being the most attractive woman you can be is fear. Your glasses, yellowing teeth, and wizened cheeks are the armor you wear to protect your emotional wounds. These less-than-pretty manifestations could simply be your defenses that shield you from the kiss that could melt your heart again. The illnesses, aches, and pains you are not dealing with could, in fact, be masking an unaddressed fear or a more serious childhood trauma. Whatever the case, they are undoubtedly holding you back from stepping out into the world with your beauty badge intact.

Cheryl, a television producer and 41-year-old single mom with one daughter, carried her negative childhood image and parental messaging with her well into adulthood. She admits it affected her choices in a mate and compromised her search for true love.

Cheryl told me, "I was the ugly, geeky-looking, overweight kid with sparkly blue glasses and frizzy hair." It took her many years to find the strength to feel good about who she was and how she looked. But once she started making changes to her appearance, starting with eye surgery and losing the glasses, it became a self-fulfilling prophecy. The more she changed her look, the better she felt about herself. Then, she went to counseling to figure out what had kept her stuck behind her blue glasses all those years. She learned that it was her defense mechanism to make herself disappear. The childhood abuse by her dad had taken its toll. Cheryl said. "Allowing people to take away my self-confidence made me feel like a doormat. I refuse to be a victim, and I will not let my daughter ever feel like I did."

You Are Your Own Worst Enemy

It took me a long time not to judge myself through someone else's eyes.
—Sally Field

Another potential death knell to your self-confidence is listening to your own internal dialogue about what you truly believe is your vision of beauty. No matter your chronological age or stage of life, your brain doesn't seem to keep pace with your body, so you stay stuck in thinking you need to look like you did in your pre-mommy era. You are certainly not that blushing bride in your old wedding photos—your past relationship and the effort you've put into raising your children has had its impact.

Be proud of what you've done, and graciously embrace your more sophisticated beauty. This is key to finding your true inner and outer game face for this stage of your life and beyond. It is critical to building and maintaining your self-esteem. By changing your internal lens to one that is kinder and gentler, you can be more receptive to the mature beauty in the mirror.

Delores, a marketing executive and 46-year-old single mother of two, has an amazing perspective on timeless beauty.

"As single moms, it's more important to feel beautiful than to be beautiful—or at least what society sees as beautiful," she says. "You have to do what it takes for yourself so that when you look in the mirror, you see the most beautiful you. This will take you much further—not just to project beauty but really take it on, be beautiful. I live in the South, and for the most part, we African-American women down here really know how to love ourselves. No matter what, we have confidence, and that feels so good. When you are a single mom, you inevitably are going to be by yourself a lot, so you have to like being with you."

Delores knows that how she sees herself has an effect on how others perceive her. She's worked very hard to create that beautiful and confident air. Her more mature version of an attractive single mom is a shining light to all the other single moms around her.

The Skin You're In

Nothing is deeper than the skin.
—**Paul Valéry**

If you wear your heart on your sleeve, then the skin on your face is your living sleeve. Your skin expresses your every joy, sadness, stress, and fear. It is the most obvious physical manifestation through which you come into contact with other living beings and the true essence of your inner and outer being. That skin on your face is your means of exercising power over people, of captivating them, of influencing their impressions and judgment, and of conquering them. *Le moi-peau,* or "skin-ego theory," refers to the idea that skin is the primary organ underlying the genesis and structure of the self. It's your most visible game-face beauty asset.

How you care for your skin is one of the ways you can express self-love. The better you care for your skin, the more positive your relationship with your body will be. Your touch and your feel will subliminally shape every relationship in your life. By taking care of your skin, you can adjust, protect, and defend yourself. You'll more easily express feelings and communicate, have fun, be active, and be in love.

Alexandra, a writer and 34-year-old single mom of three, is committed to caring for her most exposed organ: her skin.

"Skin care is a vital part of my beauty regimen," she said. "I took a few years off from really taking care of my skin when my children were little, and it showed right away. I'm back on track. My skin looks so much better now."

The Cosmetic Effect

People in every civilization have used makeup to provide protection against certain infections. Egyptians used products to care for and embellish their skin. Surprisingly, cosmetics also stimulate what is within.

Japanese scientists using a brain scanner were able to monitor brain activity to confirm that when a woman sees her own face without makeup, she anticipates how she will eventually appear to others with makeup. A "reward system" is activated, releasing dopamine and thus giving her a sensation of pleasure. In another study, when makeup was used on patients to cover severe pigmentation spots, it produced a scientifically measurable boost to their immune system. The English Red Cross included cosmetology and makeup in a hospital care program for cancer patients. The resulting boost to their self-confidence accelerated their recovery after undergoing heavy chemotherapy and radiation. Finally, when makeup was applied to the faces of senile dementia sufferers who had lost control of their sphincter muscles, they no longer needed diapers. In all these instances, makeup enabled people to recover their human dignity.

So it stands to reason that even a natural beauty might not want to bounce out of the house with a brutally bare face. Applying makeup daily is a statement about who you are, how you want others to perceive you, and how you see yourself.

Margaret, a banker and 50-year-old single mom of two, told me that it's an esteem thing for women.

"My philosophy on makeup and men is that going out for a date without your face on is like having a guy over and sleeping in ugly pajamas—you just wouldn't do it. Get Botox, do your hair, and yes, work out like crazy. Guaranteed, if you don't look good, your man *will* stray." If you don't care, why should he? is Margaret's sentiment.

She puts on makeup every day, especially as she has gotten older. "I enjoy looking good not just for a guy but for myself. It makes me feel good about me," she said.

Medical Miracles

True quality of life comes from a lasting
harmony between the body and the mind.
—Confucius

Inevitably, there are things about our bodies we cannot fix with mental perspicuity, physical fitness, or an over-the-counter product. As long as you have done all the mental work to ensure that your head is in the right place by being centered and clear about why you might want to try cosmetic surgery, then a little poking, prodding, or filling is worth the time and money.

One recent study focusing on quality of life and facial surgery found that women who lacked self-confidence and suffered from depression measurably improved their social anxiety after plastic surgery. More than 75 percent of the patients in the study reported that they felt more comfortable and confident after treatment. As the lines on their faces diminished, so did their depression. So, it is apparent that carefully considered cosmetic interventions, surgical or nonsurgical, could improve your quality of life and psychological well-being.

> Janie, a school administrator and 54-year-old mother of two, is looking forward to her beauty-enhancing surgical procedure.
>
> "Right now, I feel like a sedentary midlife menopausal woman. I've gained weight, and even though I have a really hot boyfriend right now, I don't like not feeling good about myself." She told me that it's great to have someone who loves you the way you are, but it doesn't mean anything if *you* don't feel confident. Janie is going to have a Lap Band procedure. "I think when I'm thinner, I will be moving out of this relationship," Janie said. "I'm not really much of a relationship kind of woman, anyway—I get bored easily. I think the weight has kept me stuck." Janie told me she loves feeling good about how she looks—she has a great time being flirty and thrives on the newness of a fresh relationship. Attention and adoration feed her. Janie said, "I know once I feel better and cuter about myself, I am planning on putting out that sexy energy. The surgery is the light at the end of my tunnel."

To be a well-rounded beauty and enlist all the advantages of your "beauty premium," the key is to work simultaneously on the inside and outside. Plastic surgery, skin care, and makeup cannot heal all your past emotional and mental wounds, but they will genuinely make you feel better. It can put you back on track to do the inner healing work and face the marketplace in a whole new light.

> *The difference between pretty and beautiful is this:*
> *pretty is temporal, whereas beautiful is eternal.*
>
> **—Miss Piggy**

10

SEX AND SEXABILITY

Love is the answer, but while you're waiting for
the answer, sex raises some pretty good questions.
—Woody Allen

Everyone Else Is Doing It

"The long and winding road that leads to your door will never disappear." Do you know those Beatles lyrics? Well, the winding road that leads to the door to your sex life should never disappear, either. Just because you are a mom who is currently unattached does not mean that your road should lead to vestal virginity.

Sex is good, sex is nourishing, and sex is vital. Needless to say, if you have been in a long-term sexless relationship or marriage, you've got some making up to do. You are a healthy, vibrant woman, and in spite of the fact that your hormonal drive to reproduce might possibly be waning (you've got your kids already), your desire for intimacy has not, nor should it be. In fact, it's just the opposite!

119

A study conducted by researchers from the University of California, San Diego School of Medicine and the Veterans Affairs San Diego Healthcare System found that the majority of women ages 40 to 80 years old were moderately or very satisfied with their sex lives. Their orgasms and the frequency at which these women were very satisfied with their sex lives increased with the respondent's ages. Moreover, within the month of being questioned, nearly half the women interviewed reported that they engaged in sexual activity and experienced arousal, lubrication, and orgasm a majority of the time. All of the surveys and interviews conclude that as women mature, their sex lives keep improving. We may not continue to swing from chandeliers, but we become more comfortable with who we are. We know what we like and we're not afraid to ask for it. So contrary to popular belief, even if you are solidly headed down the second-half-of-life path, your sexability is far from over.

Helen, a darling 83-year-old and single mom of two, told me that several years ago she had pretty much resigned herself to being a widow. She'd been married a total of 44 years and in that time had already buried two husbands. At 75, she had figured enough was enough. Unknowingly, the man who would soon be her beau sat beside her on a senior bus trip to Vegas. She thought he was nice looking—not handsome, but with a kind face, and she could tell he had a warm heart. He chatted her up to and from Sin City and promptly asked her out to dinner two days following their return to L.A. Within a month of their first date, they were shackin" up in her two-story condo!

"He was a sharp dresser and very romantic," Helen said. "He'd buy me flowers or candy, we went out to dinner to nice places, and he made sure I was by his side every Friday and Saturday for *shul* (synagogue)." She told me that he was very affectionate and would always hold her hand and kiss. "Were you intimate?" I had the nerve to ask. "Yes. Very," she replied. "I'm here to tell you firsthand that women are absolutely sexual well into their 70s. I didn't want a boyfriend at first, but with him, I felt like I wasn't that old and we could have a good life together." That is exactly what they did until he became ill. He died of Lou Gehrig's disease a few years ago. Now, Helen has a new boyfriend—he's 93. "And you know what?" she said, smiling. "No matter how old you get, it's nice to have some kind of connection with the opposite sex. Even at my age, there is no shortage of men. If you want to find someone, you can. They are out there!"

Sex And The Single Mom

Love is a matter of chemistry, but sex is a matter of physics.
—**Anonymous**

Clinical psychologist Dr. James Houran conducted a study about single mothers sexual attitudes and behaviors. What the good doctor discovered is that you possess what he calls "parent-engendered" skills such as selflessness, flexibility (I believe he is referring to time-management skill, not acrobatics), and stress management. All of these talents give you an edge over single women without children when it comes to a healthy sexual attitude and appetite. In fact, in his study, Dr. Houran found that single moms tended to have strong libidos and an open mind when it comes to sex.

Dawn, an artist and 48-year-old single mom of two, told me that sex is better since her divorce. Her ex didn't often initiate intimacy, and he was not passionate after she became a mother. Obviously, men like this need to shift their point of view—instead of seeing women as moms, they need to see moms as women.

"Sexuality is not predicated on motherhood," Dawn said. "People think that once you become a mother, you don't want to have sex, but that is not true." Women who are mothers are actually much freer with their sexuality. We don't want to necessarily wait for a date to have sex or do that thing we did in our 20s—not having sex when we really wanted to in order to hold out for the ring. "Being desired physically and emotionally is our aphrodisiac—simple as that," Dawn continued. "I'm not going to wait till my kids get older to fulfill that part of me."

Dawn is not letting societal mores stand in the way of what makes her feel alive and brings her sustenance—though I am sure she'll send her girls off to her former hubby's before she dims the lights and ignites the passion.

Mentalpausal

Midlife body backlash: Men go bald, women go mentalpausal.
—Kerri Zane

Having children doesn't negate the physical obstacles that can potentially obstruct your sexability as you mature. Single moms, particularly in their mid- to late 40s and early 50s, are dealing with the onset of perimenopause or menopause. This period in your life triggers your hormones. The estrogen and testosterone levels in your body go haywire. Many female research subjects have likened losing estrogen to going through a drug withdrawal. It's possible that you'll be subjected to a number of body-altering experiences you never imagined. Night sweats, insomnia, hot flashes, and an all-over-your-body drying effect can all make you feel grouchy and less than sexy.

It doesn't have to be that way. Fortunately, much of this can be managed with natural remedies such as acupressure, agnus castus plant, milk thistle, the amino acid theanine, black cohosh, fish oil, or a minimum dose of doctor-prescribed hormone-replacement therapy. Hormone replacement therapy can be a godsend, but it is also a controversial remedy. Regardless of which approach you choose, definitely discuss its viability for you with your physician.

Menopause has also been blamed for a condition called *dyspareunia*, aka painful intercourse. But the most current research indicates that this may not necessarily be true; rather, it is a result of being unaroused. Plain and simple, he's the wrong dude. If he doesn't do it for you, he just doesn't do it for you. And there is nothing titillating about the dry rub. The same researchers believe that lack of arousal affects your ability to achieve an orgasm. It's more likely that your lack of the big O is associated with psychological or interpersonal distress or perhaps the use of antidepressants, which are great when taken to get you through the painful divorce proceedings. However, the trade-off may be your inability to enjoy a new sexual partner. The good news is that menopause isn't necessarily the end of your sex life as you know it. The bad news is that if you just aren't feeling it, you are going to have to dig deeper to determine what is triggering your lack of libido.

Physical fitness also plays an essential roll in alleviating your menopause symptoms. As little as 20 minutes a day on the treadmill or taking a walk around the block will stimulate your adrenal glands, which works to convert *androstenedione,* the male hormone your body produces, into estrogen. Estrogen loss is the key factor in menopausal symptoms, and this conversion of hormones is as natural a remedy as you can get—because you produce it all on your own. Add to your fitness routine an hour to two a week of yoga or Pilates to tone, tighten, and relax your body. This in turn helps to keep your thyroid—your body's thermostat controller—on cool. An hour a day working out, preferably in the a.m. or at least three hours prior to nighttime, improves your sleep/wake cycles, which does wonders for insomnia and has been linked to lowering your odds for a hot-flash episode. So the more you exercise, the healthier you are and the milder the symptoms.

Sexability Is Your Exercise

Sex without love is merely healthy exercise.
—Robert Heinlein

A sultry side benefit of being sexually active is that the more you engage in sexual activity, the more physically fit you will be. Just as exercising releases testosterone, so does sex. The more testosterone one has circulating throughout one's body, the more muscle tissue can be built.

Regularly engaging in intimate activities also gets your heart pumping like a good workout, which increases blood flow. Blood flow is what makes your sex organs swell when stimulated and in a state of optimum responsiveness. A roll in the hay keeps your vaginal muscles fit. Just as with all the other muscles in your body, if you don't use 'em you lose 'em. They will shrink from disuse. So ladies, get your sexy on.

In addition to all these good-for-you pluses, sex can reduce stress, prevent depression, diminish anxiety, and improve sleep (you know that euphoric, relaxed feeling you get from a good orgasm—makes you sleepy, right?). Research indicates that sex may reduce your need for medication. That's because sex activates your immune system and aids in pain relief by releasing endorphins and cortisone. Because of this hormonal release, some researchers have found that engaging in sexual activity helps breast-cancer survivors recover more quickly. Consider this: Sex gets all your juices flowing, so to speak, promoting more lustrous locks, smoother skin, and heartier nails. Time to be a little less ashamed and a little more shameless.

"I never had an orgasm with my first husband," said Leslie, an office employee and 55-year old mother of four. "When my husband was finished, we were done. There was no talking, no foreplay, and certainly no vibrators. I often felt like I was left on a cliff hanging by my toes, and I didn't please myself, either." Leslie lived in that place where she thought your husband was supposed to do it all for you and you were supposed to do it for your husband. Leslie had her first orgasm at 43 years old with her new boyfriend. "I found a lot of passion had been locked up inside me for a lot of years," she said. "It was like he opened the floodgates and it all came out."

The "Tech O"

It isn't premarital sex if you have no intention of getting married.
—Drew Carey

The ability to have an orgasm is a mind-blowing awesome thing and, as we've established, good for you to boot. In technical med terms, an orgasm is the end point of the plateau phase of a sexual-response cycle. It's that intense sensation of pleasure you feel as a result of rapidly cycling muscle contractions in the lower pelvis region controlled by your involuntary autonomic nervous system. Though it may seem as if it's better for the boy than for the girl, it's the exact same process. The difference is that as the girl, you put your head and your heart into all that you do. So for you, an orgasm is the sum of an emotional, physical, and hormonal release that floods your body and brain with feel-good neurotransmitters.

Most women are unable to experience the O from intercourse alone. Women require extended clitoral stimulation. The older you get, the longer it takes—well, maybe not for everyone, but try the line with your partner and see if it works. Can't hurt! Actually, it will feel really good!

The Art of Lovemaking

If you are aroused, or if you are enjoying
someone else being aroused, you are having sex.
—Anonymous

For years, I believed, like many of the other women I interviewed, that *the act of* starts with foreplay and ends with orgasm, mostly for the guy. But whatever you call it—lovemaking, having relations, banging, birds and bees, coitus, or copulation—it is far from a straight-line journey. Your romantic interaction with another may not even include the O; in fact, it is an optional cherry on top for both parties concerned.

Authentic lovemaking doesn't come with a climax but instead happens when there is true intimacy and connection. It is one of the most important ways to create a sustainable relationship over the long haul.

> The mere fact that my REAL One and I can stand in a room full of dozens of people, look into each other's eyes, and hold an embrace without acknowledging anyone else in the room is passionate lovemaking. He'll hug me tightly and say, "I love when we make love with our clothes on." You can have sex with anyone, but you can only make love with someone whom you are truly connected.

Let your lovemaking become a metaphor for this new life you are rescripting. In this sense, go to bed with the intention of journeying with your lover to a deeper level of connection, not for the end-game orgasm. Instead of zeroing in on genitals, take the time to fully experience a leisurely and pleasurable adventure that involves every one of your senses. Then, when he finally enters you, your intercourse will be more meaningful. It will be as though he is unlocking a part of your very core that you cannot possibly reach without him. It's a place where you deeply melt into your lover, who at the same time is deeply melting into you. If you find yourself crying not sad tears but intensely powerful tears, you have reached the most profoundly intimate encounter that two people can have—a mind-blowing connection that can only happen with a total mind-body interaction.

Our bodies crave sexual connection. We are born with that yearning, but making love is an entirely different deal. It is no longer simply an act of procreation.

Josie, a senior caregiver and 49-year-old single mom of one, told me that with most men in her life, intercourse has been just a physical release and not a bonding. There has only been one man in her whole life with whom she was able to connect at this most intimate level.

"When we met, it was like an explosion of emotions," Josie said. "We had such an intense connection that when we made love, it was like he opened me up. It was as if someone touched me on the inside out. We would be locked together body to body, heart to heart, and we'd both cry. There is nothing like it. It made me happy to my soul. I feel lucky I had this man in my life. He is truly the only man I have ever made love with. He took my breath away."

Josie believes that the day you are born, your soul seeks that true connection. It comes one time, and even if that person doesn't stay with you in body, he will be with you spiritually for the rest of your life. "Unfortunately, we couldn't stay together, and he eventually married someone else," Josie told me. "To me, I feel lucky to have experienced that kind of love. My love for him will be with me the rest of my life. I may have other partners, but when I die, I will die thinking of him. I can die happy."

Josie was open to and found a man who was able to unleash the power of romantic intercourse, an experience that every woman in a REALationship can create.

If someone had told me years ago that sharing a sense of humor was so vital to partnerships, I could have avoided a lot of sex.
—Kate Beckinsale

Part Three:

THE "REAL ONE" 5

11

BE A
FLIRTY GIRL

There is no man shortage. Your dating technique needs an upgrade.
—Lauren Frances

Many women have shared that they don't know how to do it, are embarrassed to do it, or don't think they have the skills to get it done. FALSE. Flirting is an art and a science and an innately human activity. Plus, it can be so much fun! One should never fear the flirt or take flirting too seriously. In your 20s, flirting was intended to attract a suitable procreation partner. Well, you've done that partnering thing already and realized he wasn't perfectly suitable for the long haul. At this stage of the game, flirting is better described as an ongoing trial-and-error endeavor that makes the "being single" part of your life an enjoyable game of cat-and-mouse. Thankfully, scientific research implies that women worldwide are hardwired with 52 nonverbal flirty cues. Now it's time to utilize these natural gifts to ensnare your REAL One.

Flirty Science

A *Psychology Today* article stated that each of us "turns on" not to mankind or womankind but to a particular member of the opposite sex. So, while the levelheadedness and planned organizational part of the brain gets you to the party, your animal-instinct cognitive brain kicks in and goes into override once you're there. Thank goodness it does, because otherwise you might not have the nerve to look at that super-hot guy.

What happens is this: Your rational brain is always on the lookout for dangers, and it forms reasons to act or not act. This is also known as the fear's flight or fright response discussed in Chapter 3. If every time a man and a woman met they immediately considered all the possible risks and vulnerabilities they might face if they mated or had children, they'd run screaming from the room. Thankfully, flirtation's operating system kicks in without conscious consent. Get this—the moment of attraction mimics a kind of *brain damage*. Professor Antonio Damasio, M.D., from the University of Southern California, has found that people with "the damage," which occurs at the connection between their limbic structures and the higher brain, are for all intents and purposes smart and completely rational beings. However, at that moment of attraction, they become unable to make a decision or even behave rationally. Brings commitment phobia to a whole new level, doesn't it?

In attraction, you don't stop and think—you react and operate on a "gut" feeling with butterflies, giddiness, sweaty palms, and flushed faces brought on by the reactivity of the emotional brain. You suspend intellect at least long enough to propel you to the next step in the mating game—flirtation. At the moment of attraction and flirtation, your body, mind, and senses are temporarily held hostage by the more ancient part of your brain—the impulses that humans share with animals.

So you see, flirting comes already installed. You simply need to succumb to your innate instincts, let go, and put your God-given tools to the test. Don't worry—as your relationship progresses beyond flirtation and you start to date, your intellectual processes will resume. You'll be able to rationally evaluate him as a potential REAL One and decide if you want to love, honor, and cherish. But right now, you've got to make a flirty-girl choice and get started.

Online Flirty Girl

Flirting is the art of making a man feel pleased with himself.
—Helen Rowland

Forty percent of tech-savvy adults flirt via e-mail or instant messaging. They also routinely send sweet and sexy text messages by cell phone. And you can, too! Although we are all familiar with the major dating sites such as Match.com and eHarmony, you may be surprised to learn there are an estimated 1,500-plus dating sites in the U.S. to choose from and a universe of eligible men for the picking. Once you have posted your profile with your pertinents and a pretty picture, get ready for the ego stroke of your life! The winks and e-mail messages will pour in. Take a moment to bask in your feature-defining glory before you get serious and weed out the riffraff. You'll dismiss many of the guys, but a few will be standouts worthy of a thoughtful response.

Create A Picture With Your Words
When you spot a profile that you find appealing, don't just do the wink thing or use the already provided bland standard flirts. Instead,

make a statement and write him an incredibly clever e-mail. Whether you are on the phone or scripting an e-mail, the recipient will sense your energy. So, smile as you write. Exude your positivity in every communication. You are the woman who is in love with your life, so express it in an upbeat, positive way. Your communication style should be short and sweet. When you are first making contact with a new person, your discussion should be give-and-take. Really read the responses and respond to what is written. Everyone feels better when they believe the person they've engaged in dialogue is truly paying attention.

Helen, an office assistant, was a 28-year-old mother of one young son when she started dating online. She found a very interesting way of painting the picture of her world with words.

"Early on, I tried concealing the fact that I was a single mom but found that every guy I dated would become a total freakazoid when they found out," she said. So she adjusted her technique. She created a profile with an online dating service and wrote something in her profile like "I have a rock-star two-year-old who is no doubt cooler than you. If you have a problem with that, please don't even message me." She got fewer winks and messages, but the ones she got were of far better quality. She said they were interested in her and not put off by her life. Three and a half years later, Helen is still with the guy she met online. They bought a house together a year and a half ago and got married. He is an awesome standup stepdad to her now almost six-year-old. "Frankly, my son thinks my husband is way cooler than I am," Helen said.

Three Writes And He's Out

Several e-mails back and forth are important to establish initial interest, but once you've had a significant dialogue—three exchanges each is plenty—the next step should be arranging a phone call. If you don't get the "Let's chat on the phone" request and he wants to continue a writing relationship, the guy is a window shopper. And you don't want a pen pal—you want a date!

> Tracy, a schoolteacher and 51-year-old single mother of twins, told me she is an online dating pro and an expert e-mail correspondent.
>
> "First, to all my friends who are still sitting at home waiting for a date because they don't like the Internet thing—good luck!" she said. She feels that women who are anywhere near her age need to get with the program or they'll be waiting a long time. "This is the way people date now," Tracy said. "It is all about how you come across in an e-mail or an IM. I'll write them, 'Can you please get out of my head, cuz I'm trying to work.' Gets them every time!" she said.

Above all, Tracy told me she keeps the writing light, humorous, and happy. If you think the guy is interesting and worth pursuing, end your correspondence with an upbeat sign-off and a call to action for him like "Hope to hear from you soon!"

Phone-Flirty Girl

Flirtation: attention without intention.
—Max O'Rell

It's time for that inevitable first phone call—the critical exchange that leads to the first date...or not. You have to be charming, effervescent, and above all, captivating. That's no small order, but it's not that difficult. First, and most importantly, *you* make the first call, particularly with an Internet guy. Don't call from a phone that allows your number to be identified; most phone companies have you dial *67 before the number to block your number. Check your carrier to find out how to set up call blocking. Not only is it safer but it also puts you in control of when and where you have this conversation. Plus, you will never be caught off guard when the phone rings. Mental preparation for the conversation is vital for phone-flirty success.

Before you dial, there are a few things you can do to get yourself ready. Think about the conversation and how you want it to go. What would you like to tell him about yourself? What would you like to know about this guy that you haven't learned in your written correspondences? When you are ready to make the call, get comfortable. Put on your favorite music if that relaxes you. I liked to have my initial date conversations in private. I found a space that was quiet, away from my kids or anyone else in earshot. Take a deep breath, put your smile on—remember, you can hear a smile—and place the call. Bring your natural voice down an octave and stay in the positive throughout your conversation. Everyone likes being around someone who is upbeat and happy—it's not only infectious, but also very sexy.

The first thing you need to do is make sure you're talking to the right person. Immediately identify yourself and the site on which the two of you met. Be respectful of his time and circumstances. Ask him if this is a good time to speak. Allow him to launch into the first comment and let it flow. Ask about his likes and dislikes. What's his passion? Engage him in topics he really likes talking about, and be sincerely interested. Create a nice conversation rhythm just as you would volley a ball on the tennis court. Give the man time to answer, and listen to what he says. That way, you can comment back or somehow relate it to your own life and situation. If you are too busy planning your next thought, you'll miss the finer nuances. As your conversation progresses and all is going well, you can set aside rehearsed questions and ask pertinent questions that dovetail into your conversation. See if what he's saying resonates with you.

Be Yourself

Don't answer his questions based on whom you think he wants to meet. You want him to get a sense of your real personality. If you're not you, then you'll never be able to be you completely, and the relationship will ultimately be frustrating for both of you. It's okay to mention your children so that he knows you are a single mom, but don't delve into their lives obsessively. Remember, this guy wants to know about you first—later, you can talk about the other significants in your life. You can discuss your job—especially if you like what you do, books you've read, movies you'd like to see, places you've traveled or would like to see—and if you love sports or even know enough to be dangerous, you are *golden.* For some guys, the mere fact that you can honestly say you love football could be enough to motivate him to ask for the first date.

Inevitably, he will ask you how the site is working for you and if you've been on many dates. This is a strategic question for a guy to assess how picky and/or picked over you are. Your answer should always either be "you're my first" (if that is true) or "only a few." If you are the girl who books up an entire weekend at the coffee shop with new guys every 45 minutes, do it if you must, but for God's sake, DON'T TELL HIM THAT!

Wind It Down

When you feel the conversation has obvious pauses and is beginning to lose some steam, it's time to sign off. Tell him how much you enjoyed speaking with him and that you have to go. Twenty minutes for an entire first call is a good rule of thumb. If things have gone well, he's already asking you what your plans are for the weekend. You are in the driver's seat, and you get to decide whether you want to move things to the next level. Respond with an "I'm not sure—why?" Which should, in fact, lead to the first date.

No one was able to harness the power of an online romance better than Alexis, a travel rep and 45-year-old single mom of two college-age boys.

Alexis said when she wrote her online profile, she was very specific about what she wanted. "I wanted to live with a Frenchman in my dream farmhouse in the South of France," she said. That same night, she received an e-mail from her Frenchman! Despite the fact that she was living in California and he in Massachusetts, he invited her to an online chat and then an invitation to take it to the phone. They talked until dawn. Alexis said, "It was flirty and sexy, and then it was sweet and personal." They continued to talk and Skype for a couple of weeks. Then, they planned for her to fly to Boston so they could meet in person. They became engaged that first trip. "He bought me a ring before we'd even met, and it fit!" Alexis told me. She said "yes," by the way. For Alexis, it felt right even though it was fast. "I just felt like I knew, so why wait?" she said. "After all, I was not going to date a man that lived 3,000 miles away. Being engaged—that's a different story."

How's that for some inspiration! In love and REALationship, anything is possible.

Taboo Topics

Regardless of whether you are communicating in writing or on the phone, there are several topics that you should definitely stay away from. For example, don't dive into discussing feelings about your ex or ask him how he feels about his. Save it for later. Don't discuss money issues or the problems you are having with your boss at work. Don't ask about his financials or share yours. Problems with any of the above will strike chords of fear. Stay away from the universal taboo topics of politics or religion, other than to establish that both of you are okay dating each other no matter what faith and political party you subscribe to. Misspelled or grammatically incorrect flirtations are not going to score you points with anyone of substance or intelligence.

In-Person Flirty Girl

> *Beauty is power and a smile is its sword.*
> —John Ray

Seventy-eight percent of men polled say they love it when women make the first move. Nothing should be standing in your way then—it's time to exert your flirt *in puuubbblic!* To begin, scan the room with an all-encompassing glance to seek out suitable prospects. Don't stare—you just need to catch his eye long enough to make sure he acknowledges your glance. Do this a second time. The double-take confirms that you are clearly interested in making a verbal connection with him. These glances should be no longer than a nanosecond; prolonging the look takes these lightly seductive flirts into an overtly sexual realm that will send the wrong message.

The third time you catch his eye, hold his attention and hit him up with a brief but alluring smile. The duration of this third mutual eye contact will equal your level of interest in getting to know each other better. Break away from your wing women by making your way over to his section of the room and create a clear space between you and the man. This will result in an open invitation for him to approach. Recheck your target for eye contact—if he's into you, he's watching your every move. Glance and smile at him again, as this is your visual request for him to join you.

Now that you are side by side, slightly lean your body into his personal space with a comfortable one-foot-in-front-of-the-other stance. Caution: There is a fine line here between *too close* and *too distant*. You should be close enough to catch each other's scent but far enough away so that you're not looking at his tonsils when he speaks.

Then, employ the number-one fashion-forward flirty move. Pull your hair away from your eye line and toy with your tresses sporadically throughout your verbal engagement. If after your first few minutes you feel as if you want to move this interaction to the next level, try subtle shoulder dips. Lean your shoulder in toward him while tilting and cocking your head over that shoulder. Biting your lower lip at appropriate junctures will amp up the flirty "I am so into you" messaging.

They say that 70 percent of our communication is through nonverbal cues, so duplicating his actions is a surefire way of showing you are in-sync. Hold your drink the way he does. When he picks it up to take a sip, you do the same. If he's sitting facing you with his elbow propping him up on the bar, you mirror his move. He smiles, you smile back. It's subtle but effective, because imitation is the sincerest form of a compliment.

Monica, a producer and 49-year-old single mom of two, is one of the savviest flirty girls around.

"I know by a look when someone is interested in me—it's an alluring kind of eye contact," she said. She was recently in Montreal for a vacation and was sitting across the lunch table from a very handsome man. Monica was by herself. "I was the perfect target," she said. "He smiled, I smiled back, and he smiled again." She liked him and wanted to engage him, so she asked him to help her with her guidebook. "He was nice and very interesting to talk to, I had time to kill and it was fun to flirt with him," Monica said. "I ordered a coffee so we could have more time together." He not only helped her with her book—he ended up taking her on a tour. He walked her through the town and then drove her up to the top of a mountain with a beautiful view. "Then we kissed," she said. "He had a girlfriend, so there was nothing more to it than a holiday fling. But it was definitely flirty fun!"

Flirty Words

A man is already halfway in love with any woman who listens to him.
—**Brendan Francis**

Your seductress voice must be the consort of your posture and poise. Start your flirty conversation with a compliment. Use one that defines your attraction to his physical appearance, for example,

"You have amazing eyes" or "I love your shirt." Not only will you make him feel special but you also will have paved the way for him to easily kick back some kind words in your direction. Ask open-ended questions that allow him to be the authority and give you the opportunity to be enraptured by his answers. It can be anything—his job, his favorite sport, his hobby, or which bartender makes the best martini. Finally, repeat his name a few times during the course of your conversation—it's a subtle way of letting him know your willingness to create a closer, more intimate connection. A good flirt has the ability to get people to open up and talk about themselves. Not only will you get to know whether this guy is in fact a potential REAL One but also he will sense that you are interested in his thoughts. Your superior listening skills will make him feel good, and he'll remember enjoying your company.

Break The Touch Barrier

If you really like this guy, it's time to go in for the seal-the-deal flirty move. Break the touch barrier by reaching out and lightly grazing your fingertips on his forearm, shoulder, hand, or wrist. It will send a deliciously seductive chill up his spine and will also act as the ultimate signal that lets him know that you have chosen *him* to get to know better. Men respond best when they think they excite a woman. The telltale sign is in the pupils. Science has shown that the more someone likes what they see, the more their pupils open wide to take it in. The more suspicious you are, the more your pupils squeeze down. So, big, open pupils on a woman will viscerally affect a man. You can open your pupils by deliberately drawing your attention to his most attractive features.

Put it all together, and there will be no clearer signal to him that you've chosen *him*. When your conversation starts to wane, never linger. You always want to leave him wanting more. It is at this critical moment that he knows he's got to make his move and ask for your number.

Flirting is the art of making a man feel pleased with himself.
—Anonymous

12 DIVING INTO THE DATING POOL

I've been on so many blind dates, I should get a free dog.
—Wendy Liebman

Swimming With The Singles

Back in the day, all you had to do was attend your classes at school, hit a bar or nightclub, and voila—there was a host of eligible males at your beck and call. You think it's not going to be so easy this time around? "All the good ones are taken," you say. Not so. There are approximately 96 million single Americans over the age of 18, with nearly 12.6 million of those people being single parents. That's a big pool to plunge into! So honestly, it's easier than ever. Online dating is a multimillion-dollar industry. In fact, those once married are the fastest-growing group of online daters, with a 65 percent increase last year at this writing. You can literally shop for a new guy in your jammies.

Kelly, a small business owner and 46-year-old single mom of two, is a regular Internet dater. She's been on a number of sites since her divorce three years ago.

"My friends tease me," she said. "They call me The Interdater, and granted, I have had a lot of dates, but I have also had a lot of fun." Kelly told me she learned the online dating ropes through a lot of trial and error. "Pictures are the key to success," she told me. "Black and whites always get a lot of attention. But color shots look good, too, as long as they aren't shots uploaded from your mobile phone or taken in front of the mirror. Pictures are worth a thousand words, but a carefully crafted profile helps. You are in the driver's seat in attracting who or what you want into your life based on what you say."

Kelly claims that she's gone on almost 100 dates since starting her online experience. Some have been better than others, but all of them have been interesting. What she likes most about Internet dating is that she is exposed to professional men whom she might otherwise never meet. She enjoys the idea of meeting new people and having fresh experiences. That is what Internet dating offers. There is nothing more gratifying or ego boosting than signing on to your profile inbox and reveling in all the winks and blinks you receive in your daily e-mail. "One day, I received 150 responses," Kelly gloated. "It can be downright addicting, as a matter of fact. But it is especially helpful right after a divorce or separation. There is nothing that can make you feel as beautiful and desirable as a dating site."

Kelly does caution other single moms to take a lighthearted approach to the Internet search process. If it happens, great; if not, just chill. There are loads of different sites to try and plenty of men. New guys sign on every day.

In addition to online dating sites, there are a variety of professional matchmakers, not to mention all your friends and family who can't wait to hook you up. If you keep an open mind, carry on an active life, and put the word out, you will find that eligible single men are everywhere.

If you prefer to take the more traditional route to find your own REAL One, go ahead! A solid bit of advice: Do what you love or what you're interested in, and you will find like-minded men. For example, if you love photography, go to a photography class. If you want to study architecture, music, history, writing, art, or whatever it is that flips your switch, you can find a local community college class or gathering that will educate and introduce you to other people who love what you love.

As a single mom with young children, you'll be surprised how many other single parents are lingering on the playground, batting cages, or soccer field sidelines just as you are. Keep your eyes peeled for eligible males at airports, coffee shops, museums, movies, art galleries, dog parks, estate sales, or festivals. Become a volunteer for a political campaign you support. At least you'll know that you're both on the same side of the issue!

When possible, attend all the dinners, parties, and other swanky soirees you've been invited to. There may not be any available single guys there, but I guarantee that if you pipe up about your solo status, someone in the room knows someone to introduce you to.

Finally, one of my favorite ways to do what you enjoy and meet a prospective love interest at the same time is the website Meetup. com. Check it out. It has thousands of special-interest groups all over the country that cater to every activity from wine tasting to Western line dancing.

Kitty, a 26-year-old mother of twins, is a *freegan,* meaning that she practices a philosophy of nonwaste.

"Finding a man who would blend into my family and lifestyle is a little more challenging than most," Kitty told me. She and her children live in a communal situation and are dedicated to reducing the extreme waste that goes on in the United States. That means that they wear recycled clothes that are donated to the commune and gather their food from thrice-weekly dumpster dives into the trash bins of local grocery stores. Kitty joined a Meetup group of like-minded men and women, and that is where she met her REAL One. Her guy is a computer programmer by day and a freegan by night.

"We both have the same values and belief systems," Kitty said. "I know it would almost be impossible to find a man who not only gets me but wholeheartedly wants to participate on this planet the way I do. I am grateful for Meetup. I have him, my home, and a great group of friends here."

Pace Yourself

Dating should be less about matching outward circumstances than meeting your inner necessity.
—Anonymous

Often, all the friend set-ups, blind dates, website winks, nods, and notes can be time consuming. You might begin to feel overwhelmed by the work involved in the hunt. Do not let this mating pursuit become your full-time job. Only accept the invitations you are truly interested in pursuing. Respond to whom you want to respond to online. Do not feel obligated to answer everyone. We have all grown up enough to know it's about chemistry and connection. You won't hurt anyone's feelings. Don't think you have to join every interesting Meetup group you see, go to every lecture of every class you sign up for, or join 50 dating sites. Remember, there are lots of other single people out there joining your rank and file every day. There will always be someone out there looking for someone just like you.

Carolyn, a real estate broker and 58-year-old mom of three boys, designed her own unique rating system for dating following her divorce.

Carolyn said, "I categorize my men with my meals. They were either breakfast, lunch, or dinner worthy." She explained that the lunch guys are the guys you know and work with who are pleasant but whom you wouldn't want to spend more than an hour with. They are not all that attractive to you but are just people who are there. Dinner guys are the guys you really like. They're the ones you would consider spending the few hours it takes to get through a dinner and possibly sleep with them. But you'd probably kick them out of your bed before sunup. Carolyn told me, "These are the guys I would tell not to call me the next day or next week. I tell them not to send me flowers or even think a second thought about me." She went on to say that the breakfast guys are the guys you want to wake up with. They are the coffee, breakfast, lunch, dinner, and everything else guys. "They are the dangerous ones, the keepers, the ones who can turn your life upside down," Carolyn said.

Beware Of The Bad Guys

Online dating is just as murky and full of lemons as finding a
used car in the classifieds. Once you learn the lingo, it's easier
to spot the models with high mileage and no warranty.
—Laurie Perry

While you should always be cautious when meeting a virtual stranger for the first time, a truly virtual stranger—in other words, a man you've met at an Internet dating site—requires special precautions. The days of giving a guy your phone number to check his sincere interest meter are gone. You can no longer innocently allow him to call you to arrange the date, pick you up at your place, open the car door, pay for your date and politely return you to your abode with an innocent peck on the cheek.

The rules have definitely shifted my gal pals for one main reason: SAFETY. And I mean safety for you and for your offspring. When you are dating online, you have no frame of reference for the men you are coming in contact with. Dating sites are not bad for meeting people. However, new government rulings aside, these sites are not in the business of protecting you. Don't think that because a site is religiously oriented or has nothing but like-minded pet lovers on it that you are safe. BE SMART.

Within your first few initial online contacts, find out the first and last name of the man you are communicating with as well as any other basic facts such as where he works, what neighborhood he hails from, and if he also has children, what school they attend. Do a Google search to try to confirm his story. Also try to establish if you know anyone in common. It is possible that, through business or social situations, you will find six degrees of separation. Ask that mutual friend what they know about this person.

Beware if the guy is reluctant to give you any personal data. He's probably not being honest, so you need to pass on him. He may not be the guy for you. You will see when you start surfing all the many dating sites that there are pages full of eligible men. Don't feel as if the one you set free is the only one. Next! I have heard many stories from women who've gotten burned financially or worse by not thoroughly checking out their dates.

Adrianna is a talent manager and a 30-year-old single mom of one girl. An avid Internet dater, she recently met a man from Tennessee who purportedly was a real estate developer with a sizeable company in his hometown. After several months of e-mails and phone calls, they decided to finally meet in person. He took her to a romantic restaurant on top of a skyscraper overlooking the ocean. She was enamored with his Southern charm and chivalry. Adrianna thought she'd met her REAL One. When his credit card was declined and she had to foot the bill, she ignored the red flag. After dating for several more months, she sensed something fishy when they were on vacation and the waitress pronounced a last name that was different from the one Adrianna knew when the bill was delivered. Adrianna said, "I shouldn't have done it, but it was all so curious. I peeked into his wallet and found several credit cards, all with different names."

Suspicious of his intentions, Adrianna contacted a PI upon return from vacation. She kept her thoughts under wraps, as he was staying in her house following their vacation. In those six days since their return, he'd purchased a new Corvette convertible; bought new furniture, TVs, and appliances for her place; and moved her old stuff out. He was planning on making

Adrianna's house his via an old homestead law still in effect in California. "The PIs found out he had a laundry list of fraud charges on his record and was a wanted felon in three states," Adrianna said.

Fortunately, Adrianna uncovered his true identity and was able to get him out of her life before he did real damage. She cautions other single moms to do their due diligence. "There is no shame in doing a background check on someone you think you want to become serious with," she advised. "I encourage every woman to protect herself, her assets, and most importantly, her children."

Here are five very straightforward clues to help you know whether the guy you've met is who he says he is or if you should instead go back to the dating pool to fish out another:

1. **He doesn't invite you to visit his home.** Whether he lives in a mansion or a trailer home, he should invite you over. If he doesn't, it's possible that he is still married and on the sex lam or simply lives in a location he's embarrassed to reveal to you. If that is the case, you more than likely don't want to see it. Pass.

2. **He doesn't introduce you to his children.** There should be no reason that, at some point in the first six months of your relationship, he doesn't introduce you to his children. If he can't find a way for you to meet his children there is something fishy about that.

3. **He doesn't openly share all his digits.** After the first two or three months, there should be no reason not to provide you with his home phone, work phone, and cell phone. If

he insists that all contact be on his terms only, disregard any "reason" he's handing you—he's hiding something.

4. **You haven't met his best friends.** You should meet his friends because it will give you a more in-depth look into his life and character. He should want to show you off! If the two of you are always just the two of you and you're meeting in offbeat places or your house, something's up!

5. **There are certain days he is consistently unavailable.** There should be no reason over the span of the first two or three months not to see him during varied days and times. So, if Sunday after Sunday you're persona non-gratis, it's time to inquire as to how he spends his weekends. Or if a significant holiday comes up and he is not available to spend any time with his new significant other, your red flags should be flashing "Danger."

Dating is supposed to be a process by which you get to know someone, so use it for that purpose. When two available people are dating, both presumably are anxious for it to work out, are equally at risk, and are excited to learn about each other. If you sense an imbalance of vulnerability, this is your newly fine-tuned intuition at work. If he's "playing you," you will feel it. Listen to your head and not your heart at this point in the process.

You know you're in love when you can't fall asleep because reality is finally better than your dreams.
—Dr. Seuss

13 ENJOY THE JOURNEY

We come to love not by finding a perfect person,
but by learning to see an imperfect person perfectly.
—Sam Keen

I was sitting having coffee with my beautiful friend Jen a few years ago. We were lamenting the pathetic state of our dates. Jen is a gorgeous ex-model in her early 40s, a single mother of two daughters, and a power player in the world of fashion. She hangs with an attractive, fast-paced crowd and is seemingly exposed to eligible men all the time. Her dating pool should not be as shallow as for the rest of us, and yet it was. She told me that she hasn't been on a date in a while. In other words, she'd given up. "I'm focusing on my children and work instead of a relationship right now," she said. Why? you ask. Well, her last live-in boyfriend was a super-hot ex-model several years younger than she. Unfortunately, it was not meant to be. The last date she went on, the one that put her into her current state of celibacy, was with an "old man," as she described him. "He was about 10 years older than me and just had that old-man vibe," Jen said. "He was successful, which is great, but you know, he wasn't in shape. He was shorter than me and "follicly challenged." There was just no chemistry! Where are the men like me?" she bemoaned.

Like Jen, I often wondered the same thing. Where were the men like us? You know—those attractive, fit, Type-A business guys. Are all the sexy, sophisticated, successful single moms living in a "virtual no man's land" where settling for the "less than" guy is good enough? I believe you can find that perfect guy, a true love—The REAL One. The key is to not stress while on your search, enjoy your life, never lose hope, and allow your new REALationship to organically unfold. It can happen at any time and, more than likely, when you least expect it.

Adventures In Dateland

...Sometimes I get tired. Sometimes I get bored.
And sometimes all I want, more than anything
else in the world, is to go on a freaking date.
—Kiersten White

In her book *Marry Him: The Case for Settling for Mr. Good Enough*, Lori Gottlieb writes, "How disappointing it was to waste my short time on this planet in a string of temporary encounters when I could be building a lifetime of shared experience with one committed person. How much longer could I spend my time analyzing phone or e-mail messages, wasting hours talking about a guy who would be out of the picture three days, three weeks, or three months later, only to be replaced by another and another and another?" Unfortunately, many women feel the same way and end up with a less-than-perfect union; struggling through days, months, and years of enduring experiences that they will then spend the rest of their lives trying to purge from their cell memory.

Like everything else in life, the idea of dating requires a rescript. Instead of seeing it as drudgery, consider that the beauty of dating lies in this: If you don't like the one you're with, you don't have to go home with him and listen to him snore all night. If you like him, then you do get to take him home. If you really like him, then you can spend time together and discover what he's about. You can learn about his passions, and you can be treated to adventures like sailing, skiing, wine tasting, or whatever else it is this man loves to do. If you grow weary of his thing, you can move onto the next. Don't rush it. Don't settle. Certainly never compromise yourself again.

Single-mom dating is a brand-new mindset, and Crystal, a 46-year-old single mother and writer, knows how to do it right. She never gets disappointed by her dates and always makes time to meet new people. "Dating is like reading a book," she said. "People are drawn to pick up a book based on its cover. Then they'll read the reviews on the back. If they sound good, they'll move onto the inside-jacket notes. From there, they engage themselves in the chapters. But if you don't take the time to allow the story in the book to unfold, you can't fully enjoy the entire book." Crystal says the same logic applies to dating. If you only read the online profile or only allow for the 20-minute coffee date, you will never know the guy's real potential. "Is our time so precious that we can't take time for anyone else?" she asked. "I think giving your date a time limit automatically sets you up for failure."

Crystal went on to suggest that if you are on an online dating site and see a guy's picture, read the short bio. If everything checks out, then give him the courtesy of at least an hour, or go for it and have dinner. You'll be surprised what you may learn about him, about life, about scuba diving, or whatever knowledge he's garnered in his life. Plus, you'll go home with a full belly.

This One Is Younger

Age doesn't always determine maturity.
—Yetunde Odugbesan

For decades, many divorced, widowed, or otherwise mature men have chosen to connect with younger women to start second families. This in turn created a recent cultural "turnabout is fair play" phenomenon in which mature women started dating younger men. The trend picked up speed, and the moniker *cougar* was born. It is so ingrained in our lexicon that it even has a verb form, *cougaring*. Single moms who have cougared say that being with a younger guy makes them feel desirable and sexy. Hallelujah, ladies! It's now safe to date on either side of your chron digit if you so desire.

Sandy, a Realtor and 50-year-old single mom of five, found a man who sees her as a timeless beauty. She met her live-in

40-year-old fiancé eight years ago. They love each other and enjoy an amazingly solid relationship.

Sandy didn't know he was younger when she met him—she actually thought they were the same age. She told me they'd been friends for two years before they started dating, so the bond had already been solidly formed. Sandy and her fiancé have been living together for six years. "I can't imagine being with anyone else, and he is so good with my kids and me," Sandy said. "We've been through a lot. He's a total team player—he likes helping people, loves being a hero, and he's a major problem solver. He always comes up with a plan to make things better. And actually, he is the first person that my kids think of when they need advice. He's become a big part of their lives."

When Sandy found out her eldest daughter was expecting, her fiancé was thrilled with the idea of becoming a grandparent. Her daughter recently had the baby, setting in motion a relatively new and fabulous phenomenon for single moms. If you feel as though you didn't quite get it right with the man you had kids with, you have a better second chance with your REAL One as grandparents. Lots of second- and third-time-around couples are enjoying this pleasure and "having grandkids together." This time, no sleepless nights or breastfeeding!

This One Is Older

A man on a date wonders if he'll get
lucky. The woman already knows.
—**Monica Piper**

At the opposite end of the dating age continuum are the men 10 to 20 years your senior, which is where society's traditionalists would like to see you land. As a woman in your 20s, dating a man 10 or 20 years your senior doesn't seem like much of a stretch, but in your 40s and 50s, dating a man in his 60s or 70s who might be dealing with health concerns is an issue to consider.

Take Jessica, for example. A sales rep and 54-year-old single mother of four boys, she struggled financially during her marriage. When she met her wealthy current boyfriend, who is 19 years her senior, it was a breath of fresh air—until his illnesses got in the way. Jessica and her boyfriend had been friends for many, many years before they started dating. Needless to say, they have always been extremely comfortable with each other. When he became ill and went into the hospital, it just felt natural for her to be there for him. As he was recuperating, the visits became more like dates. Finally one night, she found herself sleeping over.

For the last year and a half, they've had a lot of fun. They travel together every month, and he buys her beautiful gifts. "I just feel like a princess," Jessica said. "And he's so easy to be with. He gets along with my kids, and I get along with his kids. That part is great." But Jessica went on to say that in the last few months, the medications he needs to take for his illness have taken their toll. Their sexual relationship has become virtually nonexistent. "I'm not ready for that part of my life to be over, but I'm not ready to give him up either," she said. "And why should I? Instead, I found myself what I call a "subcontractor." He's 41 years old, very handsome, and the best part is that he's a married guy who lives out of town—he and his wife don't have sex anymore. It's kind of like a mutually beneficial service call— no strings attached. You know, it's like the general contractor can't fix the plumbing, so he subs it out. My general can't do all the work anymore either."

Jessica's relationship isn't conventional, but it's not bad or wrong, either. It's just important to be realistic and consider the long-term impact your relationship choices have on all the parties involved.

Variety Is The Spice

> We waste time looking for the perfect lover,
> instead of creating the perfect love.
> —Tom Robbins

There are so many more choices and possible combinations! Some women have wholeheartedly embraced the journey and are having a great time.

For Audrey, a 62-year-old single mother of two and grandma of three, the freedom of possibilities has become an absolute boy boon for her.

Audrey told me she has different men for various needs. There is Mr. Big, 64 years old, whom Audrey's known for 15 years. "I go to his house and give him blow jobs," Audrey said. "He gives me gas money. Then there's my 36-year-old fix-it man He does what I need and then leaves at 3 a.m. I don't want him there in the morning when I wake up. I've got my routine, and

I just don't want him to see me in the morning. There is the hot young guy who is a partner in a law firm. I'm his dominatrix. He is my submissive." Her stable is rounded out with three more she's juggling from a dating service. I asked Audrey if she liked one more than the other. She thought for a moment and then replied, "I like them all. At my age, I don't believe there is one man out there who can suit me," she said. "So, I prefer to have my portfolio. I love my life right now."

Supersized Sampling

Don't cry for a man who's left you;
the next one may fall for your smile.
—Mae West

No matter which flavor you decide to taste, here's the bottom line: If you approach dating as a means to an end rather than a pleasurable journey (albeit frequently punctuated with hilarious moments), your life will pass you by and you will have missed out on all the fun.

I learned a lot about fine wines from the connoisseur I dated. I went skiing in Santa Fe—I didn't even know it snowed there! I had a sexy fling in Jamaica that was an unexpected first and spent several fabulous weekends in Hawaii—yes, with different guys, but not all at the same time. I also had drinks with a real estate developer who talked incessantly about his last girlfriend, had dinner with a guy who pulled out his coupon collection to pay the bill, and shared a cup of coffee with a guy who couldn't control his sweaty palms. Those are just a few highlights and lowlights. I've been single for 10 years, so I've had plenty of dating experiences. None of them, even when I cried because they "just weren't that into me" or simply stopped calling, ever made me want to settle for someone who was less than exactly whom I wanted just so I could be in a relationship.

As a single mom in search of your REAL One, take a chill pill and enjoy the new romance roller-coaster ride. Think about it: You have already had a spouse (or two), you have already had a child (or several) and so there should be no rush to find your REALationship. Now is not the time to be hasty and settle just to reach your goal. Goals are in the future; nothing "happens next," and it's not a destination. This is it. You're already here. Date and date some more. Laugh at the nutballs and regale your friends with stories; relish the gentlemen and enjoy the gift of their company. Think of yourself as an eternal witness to everything and everyone who enters your life. Observe the beauty in every moment. There are no extra points for reaching the end of the game first; there is only fulfillment in being a part of the play.

Even a bad date is a good story!
—Kerri Zane

14 THE 5 FINGER PHILOSOPHY

Who Is Your "Real One"

Find a guy who calls you beautiful instead of hot, who calls you back when you hang up on him, who will lie under the stars and listen to your heartbeat, or will stay awake just to watch you sleep...wait for the boy who kisses your forehead, who wants to show you off to the world when you are in track pants, who holds your hand in front of his friends, who thinks you're just as pretty without makeup on. One who is constantly reminding you of how much he cares and how lucky he is to have YOU...The one who turns to his friends and says, "That's her."

—Harry Tottszer

Right after my separation, a mutual business associate offered to fix me up on a blind date. He told me we had a lot in common—same age, both divorced, both with preteen children, and both businesspeople. He was right—we spoke on the phone and the connection was immediate. We agreed to meet at a coffee shop. The place we met sits on an unusual corner—kind of like a sidewalk promontory, so if you are walking to the door from either side of the building, you cannot see who or what's coming on the other side until you reach the double-door entrance in the center. The day we met, he approached from one side and I from the other. When we rounded the corner and met in the middle, seeing each other for the first time was like a volcanic explosion. I felt sparks fly. Suddenly, there were gazillions of butterflies rapidly fluttering their wings inside my belly. To me, he was the most beautiful man I had ever laid eyes on. I couldn't control how flustered I felt, fumbling with the change in my wallet, stumbling over thoughts and losing words. It was ridiculous. Was I in love? Or was I really just experiencing the kind of brain damage that Dr. Damasio was talking about in Chapter 10? Scrreeech, rewind.

When 75 percent of all women say they want companionship in a marriage, there should be a lot more thought that goes into picking a mate than rounding a corner, tripping over your alphabets, and boom, that's it—you've fallen in love. It's that kind of thinking that is responsible for our 50 percent divorce rate and a host of empty marriages. If a guy makes you feel like that, then chances are he is NOT your future REAL One.

The "falling in love" energy is fine for a passing flirtation, but when it comes to finding true love, your direction should be more of a rising up than a falling down. You should feel a sense of peace and contentment, a "where have you been all my life?" sort of sensibility. At this point in your life, you want to be smarter about your selection. The best way to make the right choice for The REAL One this time around is to know with certainty the type of man who will truly be the best rest-of-your-life companion for you.

Rescripting Your List

> *Every time you date someone with an issue that*
> *you have to work to ignore, you're settling.*
> **—Anonymous**

Remember 62-year-old portfolio girl and wild woman Audrey? She once posted her must-haves/must-not-haves on her Match. com profile. It looked like this:

10 musts:
- Tolerant.
- Monogamous.
- Financially secure.
- Healthy, normal sex life (but abnormal is fun, too).
- Has disability and health insurance.
- No business travel out of town or a wife in another city.
- Weigh more and be taller than me.
- Good family relationships. If you don't like your mother, you probably hate women.
- Nice car. I can't go around town in a beat-up old tank or one with big monster wheels.
- Social drinker is fine, but not an alcoholic.

12 must-nots:
- Abuse alcohol.
- Have small children or teens.

- Smoker.
- Has been married two or more times.
- Be disrespectful to food servers or bellhops.
- Be cheap or a deadbeat.
- Have a love for camping. This is a pseudonym for "I'm a cheap deadbeat."
- Have peculiar religious beliefs.
- Have large or odd pets.
- Not be tolerant of a gay lifestyle. My sister is gay.
- Have cat allergies.
- Have tattoos or metal on his face.

Audrey went on to tell me that her ideal man was intelligent and assertive, knows how to express his feelings, has a good vocabulary, loves to hug and touch, smiles easily and often, has a good attitude, is at least 50 years old, is self-sufficient—in other words, he has lived alone, can play and have fun, likes his career, is spiritual, is free of disease, has good friends and family but doesn't let them control him, is a nonsmoker, is self-aware, has plans that include me, can be monogamous, is a good listener, is free of past relationships with no ice-pick hooks that can pull him back in, is refined and respectful, has a deep voice and a strong handshake, likes to travel and wants to take me. "It's a lot," she said, "but I'll take half." I give her props—girlfriend knows what she wants. But that is a long and unflinching list, even at half. Until Audrey rescripts her list through the 5 finger philosophy, no doubt she will continue to live her portfolio lifestyle.

Does your old list look anything like Audrey's? Perhaps it's time for you to take a look at it and do a rescript too! Regardless of whether you are Internet dating, having friend fix-ups, or simply spotting a hottie at the bar, you are only getting the short story about that person but not the *real* story. You will know if the guy is a doctor, a lawyer, or commander in chief, but you'll have no clue as to whether he has integrity, keeps commitments, or will be considerate of your children. You will neither know the man nor understand what's important to you.

Take some time to dig inside yourself and figure out what lies behind the *why* of your choices on your old list instead of just accepting them at face value. Use those discoveries as reference points to rescript your new list. Ask yourself if you really must date a lawyer or if you want to be with someone who is grounded, lawyer or not. Do you really need to have a man who will go to chick flicks with you, or is it that you are looking for a guy who is in touch with his emotions—a guy who will listen to your feelings and share his with you. Does it matter that he has a full head of curls, or is his hair count more of an ego trip about how you see yourself?

If you can explore the underlying reasons for your old choices and update them through a new point of view, then perhaps you will have a better barometer of what your new-and-improved list is. By drilling down to your real wants, you will discover a brand-new universe of available men. Plus, it is your opportunity to seek out what real companionship chemistry means for you. Then you'll be able to make a better choice based on who you really are and what is really important to you.

Janice, a physician and 39-year-old mother of two, is absolute in her rescripted-man list.

"My list is becoming very specific," she said. "I've erased any particular image of what this man should look like, and I prefer now to think in terms of character, values, and honor." Janice's list includes a man who is honest—someone who can live by his word and understand the impact of his words. Her man will be someone who lives by his values and can be respectful of her and her children. She is confident she can find it all in one man, and she emphatically told me she is not going to settle. "I believe that God works through odd channels and he is going to deliver the right man when I'm ready to receive him," she affirmed.

Janice was recently presented with a man who is a bald Southern marine, a redneck with a loud voice and plenty of muscles. Instead of dismissing him right away as she would have in the past, she let herself listen to him. The more she listened, the more she liked him. He seemed very wise and honorable. "You really can't judge a book by its cover," Janice said. "I'm not certain that he is the one, but I am going to continue to work through this one and see where it takes me."

Janice is clearly using the 5 Finger Philosophy to look at her new man. It is the most quantifiable, absolute, and irrefutable method for finding not just *the* one, but The REAL One.

The 5 Finger Guy

Dating should be less about matching outward
circumstances than meeting your inner necessity.
—Anonymous

Each Finger of the 5 Finger Philosophy represents a key quality that is important to single moms. Why five fingers? Well, metaphorically speaking, when you are holding hands with a man and you lock two fingers together, your hold can easily break apart. It is similar for three and four fingers. But when you lace all five fingers together, you have an invincible hold.

Don't worry if a guy you've met doesn't fit your 5 Finger Philosophy like a glove right away. A 5 Finger REALationship is a work in progress. For example, if you can definitively establish that you match up on three of the five, share your philosophy with him, and the two of you can work together on syncing up the rest. They don't need to be matched up in any particular order either, just as long as you ultimately work through each to a complete rock solid five-finger hold.

First Finger: Physical

Abundance can blossom as we shift our perception.
—Wayne Muller

As a more mature adult woman and single mom, the attraction in a mate becomes less about his physical surface and more about his physical substance and body feeling. Eye color, height, and quantity of hair take a backseat to how a man takes care of himself, how he takes care of you, and how you feel physically when you are in his presence. It is also important to have the same level of commitment to exercise and fitness. In other words, you don't have to do the same activities, but your desire and interest for overall health and well-being should match.

Had I gone solely by my old list, I would have questioned if my guy could possibly be my REAL One based simply on the photo presented to me. Instead I went into my first date with an open mind. From the moment I saw him in person and we hugged, it was a body feeling and compatibility that took over. Fortunately for me, he is tall and handsome, but it was that mystical chemistry combined with the sense of peaceful knowing I felt with his embrace that had me immediately realize the physical finger was there for us.

Hobbies are great, especially if you enjoy the same activities, like golf or reading. It's not necessary that you have exactly the same interests as long as you do have interests other than just each other and respect each other's time to participate in them.

Another critical physical factor for single moms is a man's independent financial resources. You have your children to support, and that is plenty. Now is not the time to take on another fiscal responsibility. He should be secure enough to be self-reliant but generous enough to treat you like a lady. He should have a stable living situation. He should be a caring and monetarily responsible dad to his children or grandpa to his grandchildren.

Finally, he should understand and be compassionate about the role you play in your children's lives. He has to be clear that, no matter what, your children are not to be supplanted as the most important people in your life.

All this is not to say that chemistry is a moot concern. Your pheromones are alive and well, and your olfactory senses are still vibing. So, just let your subliminal self be your guide in that department.

Loretta, a retired 80-year-old single mom of three, had some sound words of wisdom.

"I gravitated toward strong men," she told me. "I like a man who is a man and can step up and make decisions. More than looks, I wanted him to be caring. I would look to see if he would be a good a father and stepdad. He needed to be financially secure and not a miser. That is a really big no-no. It's very important that he be generous with me and all the children—mine *and* his."

Desiree, the 46-year-old single mother of a son with cerebral palsy, echoed Loretta's sentiments.

"The most important criterion is how he responds to my son," Desiree said. "I look to see if he is the kind of person who patronizes him or treats him like a regular person. It takes a unique person to be in a relationship with a single mom who has a special-needs child. A man who can keep his word is important. I like someone who cares about his physical health—someone who is financially self-sufficient, not in debt, and happy in what work he does. I look at the friends he keeps and how he treats people. Of course, the ability to laugh, listen to good music, and have a good time is key."

Second Finger: Mental

Real humor is the synthesis of joy, wisdom and compassion.
—Roberto Assagioli

Your 5 Finger guy should be your intellectual equal. He should stimulate your mind as brilliantly as he arouses your sex organs. After all, a woman's brain is the most powerful seductress. The two of you should be able to seamlessly spend hours in bed or on the couch engaged in an engrossing mental volley. It helps to laugh together and have a sense of humor about life. In other words "don't sweat the small stuff."

Mutual respect is important. Ultimately, you want to choose a man who will always be your friend. While you are spending time together, consider whether you could still have this guy in your life if the sexual intimacy in the relationship dissipates. I am not saying that this is what you want. But processing through that thought will help you determine if this guy qualifies as a true companion. When you and he are mentally compatible, the capacity for sustaining a long-term relationship rises exponentially.

One test that allows you to know is whether you can honestly say you're able to be "together alone and alone together." What that means is, can just the two of you go out to dinner or on a vacation, or do you need other couples to join you? Likewise, can you simply sit alone quietly reading while your REAL One does the same and just be in that space for hours?

Kaitlin, the 41-year-old mother of two in the throes of a gut-wrenching divorce, was very clear about her rescripted man list.

"Next time around, I am not going for looks or money," she told me. "I don't care a pip about that stuff. I had lots of money when I was married, and he left me without a penny. So, why should that matter? I want someone who's got a substantial basement. Someone I can talk to who has something interesting to say. Someone who will listen to what I have to discuss, too. I am not open for a lot of compromises. If I feel the least bit uneasy about a person, I am not brushing off my intuition anymore. I am very in tune now with what I want, and my antenna is up fully. It has been so darn difficult to reach freedom—I will not compromise again."

Third Finger: Emotional

Our love is not about being lovey-dovey; it is about an adult commitment to dealing directly with our feelings and concerns.
—**David Richo**

The emotional Finger is a very important one and is critical for a lasting connection. At the top of the emotional heap is trust. You've undoubtedly learned from your last relationship that if there is no trust, little else matters. When you can trust your partner on every level, you can open up and be completely vulnerable to him.

Trust can only come from constant communication. Authentic communication is built on talking and listening. This is heartfelt listening in which you quiet your mind and really pay attention. Don't just hear his words—listen to his actions and body language as well. It is how and what he is being that is truly important. He should be able to open up to you about what his fears are so that you can talk them out. He is a man who must be completely present and in the moment with you, appreciating all you bring to him in your shared space and time. And he is the guy who sees your world as complementing, not completing, his own.

Be completely in tune with this special type of guy. You both must learn to be completely honest with each other and take responsibility for your words and actions. Even if it is something you think he doesn't want to hear or know, or vice versa, it should be voiced. No secrets and no hidden agendas are requirements for building 100 percent trust.

There needs to be an unyielding commitment you make to each other. You must both be willing to handle any issues that come up between you by addressing, processing, and resolving them before they become insurmountable conflicts. In other words, state the issue and then process your individual thoughts together. Work through it methodically and patiently until you arrive at a mutually agreeable resolution (not necessarily a compromise). Revealing your inner feelings to another person is what makes you the most vulnerable. Only in being completely vulnerable to each other can you achieve absolute trust and commitment. Contrary to what you might think, complete vulnerability is what makes your relationship stronger.

Sharing feelings openly will ultimately allow for validation of your thoughts, which is what's required to feel loved. Your REAL One should provide a safe space and mirror those thoughts for you without taking anything personally. By doing so, he can lead you to your true self in a way nobody else can. Number two of Don Miguel Ruiz's Toltec-based book of wisdom, *The Four Agreements,* is "don't take anything personally." Easier said than done, but realizing it is half the battle. You can also show a playful but still caring side by sharing your feelings with cards, love letters, or surprises when least expected (not just on holidays and birthdays).

Trust is earned and happens over time, so pace yourself with this one. It's not going to happen overnight. As you get to know him and hopefully find that he lives with integrity, your emotional bond will strengthen.

Rebecca, a retail manager and 26-year-old single mom of one daughter, found the ability to trust again in her new man.

"I was 24 years old and engaged for almost three years when my ex and I split up," Rebecca said. "During those three years, he fathered three additional children with two other women, which eventually led to the end of our relationship. One month later, I met one of the most handsome men I had ever seen. He was gentle with my feelings and very understanding. He worked hard to let me know I could trust him because he knew I was in a real bad place due to the events that had transpired during my previous relationship. Almost one year to the day of meeting this new man Rebecca became engaged and nine months later they married. "He has been honest with me from the beginning, he never tried to impress me, we've always been ourselves, and I feel comfortable being ME around him. I realized he liked the real me. He helped me to be a better person professionally and personally," she said.

Fourth Finger: Spiritual

Spirituality is the thoughtful love of life, but ultimately it must also be understood in terms of the transformation of the self.
—**Robert C. Solomon**

The spiritual Finger goes beyond simply matching up your religious denomination, beliefs, and practices. These are all good concepts to discuss, and certainly, the more aligned you are in all these areas, the easier it is. However, there is so much more to a man's spirit. Does he really know you, and does he really know himself? Has he done work similar to what you've just completed? Has he cleared his past stories and rescripted or transformed his life to be open to a future with you? He must be a man who is at peace with who he is and where he is in his life. You want him to be clear about his wants and have the ability to set aside any of his self-absorbed needs. He should be the kind of man who can be completely open and authentic to his core about who he is.

Spiritual compatibility includes basic values and beliefs and the way in which each of you experiences the world. Get a pulse on his level of compassion, spirit of cooperation, tolerance of others, and commitment to making a contribution to this planet. The closer these aspects align, the better you'll be able to build a solid foundation for your relationship. Study together—read passages that you find important and see if they resonate within your partner. Discuss all your thoughts on what you both uncover; it will help to clarify and refine your values and beliefs. The goal is to always want to grow independently and integrally.

Dori, the 41-year-old four-time cancer survivor and single mom to a special-needs child, included a heaping dose of spirituality on her man list.

"I am not concerned about physical image—I'd rather connect with someone who seeks self-help," Dori said. "I want to be with someone who is interested in always studying and growing or at least open to the thought of that. He should be successful—not rich, but wanting a better life. Somebody who wants to take care of me and have me take care of him. I'm old fashioned—if I'm going to play house, I want to be in the role."

Fifth Finger: Sexual

When he looks into your eyes, you feel him entering your heart.
                    —David Deida

A fulfilling complete sex life is integral to all the other aspects of your relationship. For single moms, this fifth Finger is the pinnacle of your physical, mental, emotional, and spiritual Fingers. You and your potential REAL One should be able to come together to bring each other the natural joy of lovemaking and the ultimate ecstasy of an orgasm, as described in the Art of Lovemaking in Chapter 13.

Almost any two people in a relationship can strip their clothes off and achieve the Big O, but that alone does not make for a genuine love. You are looking for true connection, a deep physical type that lovemaking provides. As David Deida points out in his book *Dear Lover: A Woman's Guide to Men, Sex and Love's Deepest Bliss,"* as a young woman you dreamed of being lovingly taken by a man you could trust with your life —a man you could trust to take you to a profound place of opening. In order to have this kind of connection, you must master the unique bond that can only be achieved through lovemaking. Deida says, "True sex is about divine intimate communion, heart-to-heart worship, opening as love's bliss, offering your deepest gifts to each other. This two-bodied sexual offering prepares you for opening beyond yourself so you can offer your deepest gifts in every moment to all beings, opening as love's light through every body."

What this means is when you are in your childbearing age, biology takes precedence, and sex or lovemaking becomes mostly about the goal of procreation. Once you have had your children that is no longer a primary need, and lovemaking becomes more of a desire for an immersive connection between two people that can lead to ultimate fulfillment. It is when you are able to achieve this level of sexual connection that you've mastered the most unifying and truly elusive of the Five-Fingers. It is invigorating, exciting, enveloping, healthy, and optimum for your self-esteem and absolute satisfaction. It's the key to achieving a long-term human REALationship.

Anne is a publicist and a 43-year old widow and single mother of two teens. She has found this exquisite kind of connection with her new beau.

"My guy and I just had our one-year dating anniversary," Anne said. "He's got a rough and sexy job as a transporter, but he is patient and romantic. He is so good about holding and rubbing hands, kissing so passionately, and hugging tightly. It is sharing those feelings that makes you believe that you are one… so connected…I think of him every day, and we see each other almost every day. We miss each other when we are apart. We always have a lot of laughs no matter what we do! That's how I know he's the (REAL) one! Yes, I'd love to be married to him. I feel this is where we are heading."

And I am happy to report that, during the writing of this book, Anne became engaged to her REAL One.

People are happiest when all aspects of their lives are congruent with their overall goals. We single moms have experienced that the erroneous idea of *any* marriage being good enough for us to be happy is simply *not true*. REAL companionship is the goal and finding the perfect Five-Finger REAL One to spend your life with is your key to joy and fulfillment.

Meeting you was fate, becoming your friend was a choice,
but falling in love with you was beyond my control.
—**Anonymous**

15 ROCK, PAPER, HEARTS

You know it's never too late to shoot for the stars
Regardless of who you are
So do whatever it takes
Let nothing stand in your way
Cause the hands of time are never on your side.
—**Nickelback**

Here we are at the apex of your authentic love potential. You have been empowered by all the knowledge and skills to rescript your life. You are able to better understand yourself, better understand him, let your self-confidence shine, and rally support from everyone around you. If both you and he have your hearts and your heads in the same place, you have achieved true love. Congrats! You're involved with The REAL One. Now you have to decide how you will let your romance play out for the rest of your life. Will you BE together in the happily-ever-after REALationship, or will you choose to once again tie the knot? Or both?

Making the best decision—that is, to marry or not marry this time around—requires thought, consideration, and knowledge. Having a full understanding of the origins of marriage—where it's been, where it's going, and why it doesn't work for everyone—might help you as you move forward in a dynamic and lasting long-term REALationship.

The Genesis Of Marriage

...Because marriage doesn't work in the world today. It's an institution that is in decay. And if I have love I wish to portray, I will surely find another way.

—Sublime, "Ball and Chain"

The naissance of the marriage contract was first and foremost as a financial arrangement. Anyone who's gone through a divorce can attest to that fact. When it comes down to brass tacks, the deal is the deal. Adding the emotions is what makes it messy.

The formal union between a man and a woman—a marital contract—appeared in Hammurabi's Code, recorded around 1790 B.C. The Code's marriage laws don't hold with our current belief that marriage is the result of love and romance. Instead, it was a business bargain with the family of the bride and had specific rules for fidelity, bearing of children, and amassing property. There were also a number of laws within the Code to protect paternity—with sufficient cause, because there were no paternity tests back in the B.C. Without having any type of control over "his woman," a man might have worried that the child she was carrying might not be his. Therefore, he had no way of guaranteeing that his true bloodline would inherit his wealth and property. Under the Code's rules, women were given to believe that the man they "married" would care for them and their children.

But the Code included an out-clause for the guys, indicating that in the event his wife was barren, he could ask her to bring him a maidservant to bear his children. Besides being a wife and mother, women had few choices as to profession outside being vestal virgins, prostitutes, or tavern keepers. This isn't to say that the Code had no rights for women, but ultimately, unless he'd done her dire harm, a woman was beholden to her husband. This kind of arrangement smacks of enslavement rather than healthy partnership.

Somewhere along the way, women became convinced that marriage was an institution created to protect them. Women believed that if a man professed his love and showed up with a circular band to slide on her finger, it was tantamount to his lifelong commitment to her best welfare and his fidelity.

And the church-along with the brothers Grimm-did their best to perpetuate the illusion that marriage was a fantastic, pure, and sacred place for men and women to reside.

Jocelyn, a fashion designer and 44-year-old single mom of one, is not a proponent of signing on the nuptial-contract dotted line.

"I'm not interested in it," she said. "I am pretty confident that women can have happy relationships without changing names. I don't see any reason for it." There is, in fact, no need. The essence of any solid relationship is simply to be good to each other. But tradition has embedded the institution in our psyches. Religions push the practice from generation to generation. Jocelyn thinks the whole concept of marriage is nonsense. Many of her friends are married and unhappy, and no one really knows how life will play out over time. What someone wants today may not be what she wants 10 or 15 years from now. "Why tie yourself up that way?" Jocelyn asked. "For me, I don't want to get involved. I have four businesses—I'm very busy. Until I meet someone I truly desire, someone I can have healthy conversations with, I'm living solo, like my role model, Oprah."

Prince Charming: RIP

Don't cry because it's over—smile because it happened.
—Anonymous

You've read the fairytales and grew up buying into the fact that you were entitled to a Cinderella-like romance followed up by a grand wedding. There is the requisite knight in shining armor who hunts you down on his fabulous white steed, picks you out of the crowd, and saves you from your sad, single maiden existence. There is all the fun and high expectation in planning the glorious connubial event. You see spectacular dreamlike images of yourself in the perfect white dress, the adoring friends and family nodding and smiling as you walk down the aisle. You imagine the reveling and pure ecstasy at a kickass after-party! You just blindly believe that *happily* is an automatic extension of *ever after*.

Honestly, can't we all look back now and see there was no way for us to know what that was supposed to look like? There is no storybook fairytale of how to live with the person in the tux waiting for you at the end of the aisle after the blush of bridedom slowly fades to black. There is just no foolproof Happily Ever After guidebook! With a divorce rate at nearly 50 percent, it is increasingly more apparent that being married is not the penultimate state of happiness. In a

15-year study, researchers found that a person's happiness level before marriage was the best predictor of happiness after marriage. In other words, getting married doesn't automatically flip the happy switch. So why do you think that marriage is the be-all-end-all? Why do you believe that if only you were married, you'd be happy? A beautiful wedding does not guarantee happily ever after.

Lori, a journalist and 46-year-old single mom of two daughters, is shifting her focus from the *real* wedding details to the *REAL One*.

"I loved planning my wedding," she said. "All the details were perfect—the right location, the best dress, the most delicious food. I remember walking down the aisle loving how every detail turned out. Then I thought I shouldn't be doing this, but if I don't go through with it, how am I going to return all those boxes?" After the ceremony was finished, the rabbi asked the couple if they wanted to spend their first few minutes as husband and wife alone together. Lori didn't want to. She knew the food at the reception was good, and she was hungry. At that moment, it dawned on her that she shouldn't have felt like that. The marriage wasn't on solid footing then or ever. After 15 loveless, mentally abusive years, she knew she didn't want to live that way anymore.

Leaving her marriage was an exciting adventure, and she was ready. "I see now that there is no expiration date on life," she said. "I can do whatever I want anytime. I have a new support system in all my other single divorced-mom friends, and I no longer feel like I need to depend on anyone. I never want to feel trapped again, and that is what I'm teaching my daughters: to be independent."

As Lori realized, marriage can foster a false sense of ever-after security. It can breed complacency and an unhealthy codependence. In truth, any long-term relationship cannot be a panacea of happily ever after if not initially engaged in from the right frame of mind. Women make better choices from a place of confidence, self-assurance, and autonomy. Knowing that you are physically, mentally, emotionally, spiritually, and sexually independent will allow you to take full responsibility for your life for the rest of your life. The best relationships don't come from a place of codependency but rather from interdependency.

The Mrs. Mouse Trap

> *You don't have to be married to have a*
> *good friend as your partner for life.*
> —Greta Garbo

Author Diane E. Babcock says, "A marriage license does not contain the word "kill." *Till death do us part* should be taken as death of the marriage, not of a person. Marriage is not a purpose in life—life itself is purpose that may or may not include marriage. Marriage may happen once, several times, or never in a lifetime and may last hours, days, months, years, or decades. You may be gun-shy after the first one and dance around it for years. Marriage is not the ultimate in life—love is and marriage becomes a curse without it."

It seems that it's time for our society to gracefully accept that a small portion of the traditional wedding vow needs to be modified with a more pragmatic "Till whichever occurs first, divorce or death, do us part."

Cynthia, a finance executive and 57-year-old twice-divorced single mother of four boys, believes marriage is old school. Happily cohabiting with her man for the last five years, she has no plans to tie the knot. Her reasons for steering clear of the paper sound well founded.

"Marriage is an antiquated system," Cynthia said. She has always believed that the purpose of marriage is for two adults to come together to create a whole and provide a home in which to share the responsibility of raising children. When the commitment to each other in the marriage is broken, there is a loss that is irreplaceable. Staying married to a person you don't love anymore in order to keep the family whole actually creates an environment that is an empty chasm for those little beings you love. "For me, the commitment to marriage is not as important as the commitment to raise healthy, whole kids," Cynthia said. "We don't need a legal contract for that." She and her new boyfriend have agreed not to marry. They believe that blending families is a misnomer. "More often than not, trying to foster the Brady Bunch creates competition and conflict," she told me. "We each have our children, his two and my four, and our sole focus is on each child's well-being. Getting married isn't going to make that commitment any stronger."

Cynthia is not the only one who believes the concept of matrimony has run its course. With people living a lot longer, couples may have up to an additional 50 years to live together once they are empty-nesters. This has lead to a new trend in which one in four divorces in the U.S. in 2009 was by people ages 50-plus. This is up from one in 10 in 1990. Equally important to note, two out of three divorces for people over 40 years old, are being initiated by women.

The statistics clearly indicate that these couples, and in particular women, believe that rather than spending their lives in unfulfilling marriages. They'd rather have their freedom. When interviewed off the record, the most common reason people state for the dissolution of their marriage was cheating!

Cheating Is A Lie

The moment you possess a living being you have killed that person.
—Osho

The propensity for cheating occurs as a direct correlation to the lack of honest communication in a relationship. It has been scientifically proven beyond a doubt that humans are not meant to be monogamous. Further, as we uncovered in Chapter 13, sex and intimacy or lovemaking are two entirely different states of being. You can have sex with anybody, but you cannot have a relationship with just anyone. The distinction is your ability to have true intimacy—in other words, verbally communicating openly and honestly as a couple. The fact that you or your man might be interested in a little sexual variety should be discussed. You can both allow for honest discussion about fantasy, realizing that neither of you can satisfy every desire for the other. By providing a safe place to share those thoughts with each other, there is no deception, and thus the concept of cheating becomes moot. Take it a step further and establish predetermined parameters for how those sexual proclivities will be handled.

My REAL One and I call this our "sexual standard." We've each committed to behaving exactly the same way we would when we are not together as we do when we are together. In other words, in any given situation, I will behave as though he were standing right there with me. Moreover, I provide a safe place for him to look at other women and share his thoughts, as I do looking at other men. I also proactively suggest he go to gentleman's clubs with me or with his friends. For us, it has assuaged any sexual desire to go outside our relationship and it gives us no reason to lie to each other.

If there were a situation in which an external sexual encounter did occur, it would be a rare and spontaneous situation. As we've agreed, our commitment is that it would never result in a relationship with another person and most importantly never could threaten our love for each other. With this level of knowing, all jealousy simply dissipates and gives us a greater chance for healthy maturity in our relationship. As adults, all that really matters is enduring mutual respect and understanding.

In his book *The Mastery of Love*, Don Miguel Ruiz supports the described approach. He suggests that partners in a romantic relationship should take the risk and create an agreement that works for them, "not an agreement that you read in a book, but an agreement that works for you. Use your imagination to explore new possibilities, to create new agreements based on respect and love." He goes on to say, "Communication through respect and love is the whole key to keeping the love alive and never getting bored in your relationship. It's about finding your voice and stating your needs. It's about trusting yourself and trusting your partner."

Michelle, a 46-year-old sales executive and single mom of one, regrets her response to her ex's "cheating."

"Why do we fight what is innate?" Michelle asked. "While I was pregnant, my son's father had sex with his ex-wife. It was a purely physical thing for him. The intercourse meant nothing to him emotionally, but to me it was betrayal He was a good guy in many, many ways and I tossed him out—while I was pregnant with his child, mind you—for doing something that is just part of a man's DNA," Michelle said. "To me, I compare 'cheating' to the analogy of taking drugs. When something is taboo, there is a mystery about it. When it's allowed, the allure dissipates. If women would allow men to be men and women be allowed to be women, I think we'd all get along better." Michelle has a twin sister who is in an open relationship. Her sister and her husband both have agreed that either may have sex with other people. "Neither of them has done it, and they've been married for 20 years," she said. Michelle's sister recognizes what her husband needs and lets him understand she knows what he needs diffuses his desires. "It works for them," Michelle said.

So, is it time to rescript your interpretation of cheating and the definition of a significant relationship? Though counterintuitive, the ability to share and openly discuss your sexual interests or fantasies with each other will make your relationship stronger.

Ultimately, if you and your partner have completely open communication about sexual fantasy and a strong sexual connection but you or your man is still interested in secretly straying, this is a symptom that something about your relationship that isn't working, and it could be time to move on.

Matrimony, Monogamy, and Monotony: Nothing lasts forever

As far as the present and the future are concerned, marriage is absolutely irrelevant, inconsistent with human evolution and contradictory to all the values we love: freedom, love and joy.
—Osho

The traditional marriage protocol creates an unnatural constraint of monotonous monogamy for both parties involved and a virtual breeding ground for contempt and jealousy. It takes an extraordinarily lucky human being to live virtuously within the confines of the marital rules till death do us part, particularly as human life span increases. Research has indicated that the human mind was not made for monogamy. In her book *Why We Love: The Nature and Chemistry of Romantic Love*, anthropologist Helen Fisher reported that sexual wanderlust is in fact a symptom of our biology. Her research showed that humans aren't meant to be together forever; instead, she suggests we opt for serial monogamy or multiple soul mating.

Serial monogamy offers several relationship benefits in that it can relieve the potential monogamy monotony. With the ending of each relationship, you become a stronger and more confident partner for your future relationship. Having a few relationships under your belt helps you to become more mature. You will learn what you want and don't want.

With this in mind, I suggest you consider a more controllable commitment pact. You both can agree to stay together for the short term, which could be 12 months, 5 years or 10 years. Then, renegotiate the terms of your commitment when it comes up for renewal. The two of you can always agree to stay together term after term, or for whatever reason, you can opt out with the pre-negotiated deal already in place when your term completes. It keeps the relationship dynamic fresh in addition to being manageable and rational. Best of all, it is just between the two of you and nobody else.

Lets All Conjugate

A soul mate is the one and only other half of one's soul, which every soul should find and join. It is a person with whom one has a feeling of deep and natural affinity, love, intimacy, sexuality, spirituality, and compatibility.
—**Anonymous**

Although marriage is not the right choice for everyone anymore, sharing your life with someone, should you so choose, is eternal. A friend once said that humans are conjugal beings. In other words, we have an innate need for love and connection. According to interpretations of the Kabbalah, the compulsion to find a soul mate is an expression of the human soul's deepest ambitions. Mystics explain that two primary considerations drive the soul's desire to mate: one is to be complete and the other is to transcend itself. One interpretation of Genesis is that Adam and Eve were initially created as a single two-faced body. The single being was split in two—a man and a woman. In the world of souls, the partition and reunification of the male and female components of individual souls occurs continually. So, despite your divorce or loss of a beloved, the all-important quest for a soul mate is a timeless, lifelong endeavor. What you may not have considered is that soul mates come in many varieties and serve various purposes at different times in your life.

Jill, a publicist and 27-year-old single mom of one, believes in the power of the soul mate but not necessarily the power of a singular romantic soul mate.

"I don't believe in romantic soul mates," she said. "I think that many souls find connections. There might be a soul sister that I don't know about, or a parent and child who "get" each other so well, they are soul mated." The search for a romantic soul mate gives people an excuse to fall in love. Jill believes that relationships are about chemistry, communication, and working with each other to make it work. "Being my soul mate is too lofty—there is no man who can "complete" me," she said.

Being a single mom doesn't mean you failed. Like Jill, you will undoubtedly find one or more new soul mates in your lifetime. Perhaps a healthier, more realistic, and more successful approach to a loving and long-lasting relationship is one in which you and your partner grow to become soul mates. Science agrees. When measuring the brain activity of couples 20 years into their marriage, 90 percent of couples who married for love, long-term commitment, and companionship had lost the passion they originally felt. In other words, they became less "in love" with each passing year. Couples who came together in arranged marriages found their love grew steadily as the years progressed. I am not suggesting you rush out and find a matchmaker to hook you up. However, rather than falling in love and getting married as you've done in the past, consider rising in love with a 5 Finger REALationship and have a lifelong renewable commitment. Marriage doesn't equate to soul mate, and having a soul mate doesn't require marriage.

"May I please have a large order of love—and hold the side of paper!" For me, I would rather have my man's heart and his respect and knowing, caring, and companionship for the rest of our living days than the big sassy diamond on my left ring finger and his signature on the bottom of a marriage certificate. I'd prefer to know with certainty that he wants to be by my side because it's his choice to be by my side, and likewise, my choice to be by his. I've learned that there is no piece of paper or promissory note that can guarantee that level of commitment. What I am sure of with my man is that if there is nothing legally keeping him in my universe and he's still around—I am truly loved.

Many people seeing my REAL One and me together just assume we're married. When they ask if we are, our response is that we are married spiritually. It is our spiritual commitment to each other that we'll be together as long as we continue to grow individually and mutually. And your spirit is truly everlasting.

> *Seduce my mind and you can have my body,*
> *find my soul and I'm yours forever.*
> **—Anonymous**

Final Thoughts

Let your soul direct your heart and your heart direct your
body. Only then will your body, heart, and soul soar!
—Kerri Zane

Regardless of the circumstances that led you to single motherhood, the outcome of the experience no longer needs to be traumatic. Having engaged in the process of rescripting your life, improving your inside-outside, and putting the 5 Finger Philosophy into practice, you've obtained the wisdom and fortitude to handle any of the challenges that may come your way. You are now a strong, emboldened, enlightened, and more confident woman who is ready to step into a healthy and meaningful relationship with your REAL One and have a REALationship.

So your childhood might not have been picture perfect and your starter family didn't turn out to be Ozzie and Harriet. None of that matters. The twists and turns you took on your road to now were not fatal errors but rather directions on the path you chose to take. Now it is time to create your new living vision, take another turn, and make a different choice. You know that the only way to overcome your fears is to face them straight on, saying yes to every perceived obstacle (aka opportunity) and then living the rest of your life with no regret.

You have the opportunity to fully embrace who you are and how you are being. You no longer need to listen to the negative chatter in your head talking you into the ground. You have the skills to drown them out and talk yourself onto a self-proclaimed and well-deserved pedestal. There is no waiting for tomorrow when all you need is right here, right now. The best opportunities are for savoring in your flow. Undoubtedly, true love *will* show up, but while you are on the roller-coaster ride of your life, enjoy the journey. Bestpectations abound!

With a head full of joy and a positive outlook on life, your balancing act will look less like a haphazard battleground of misplaced yeses and more like a carefully coiffed boundary of no's, with a little extra time on the side. You will have sound negotiating strategies at home with your kids and your ex.

You have learned all the reasons for taking extra-good care of your physical appearance. It is all *so* good for your mind, soul and, of course, your body! All these accomplishments prepare you for that essential opening to finding not just *the* one but The REAL One. There is nothing stopping you from hitting the scene, whether online or in person, to search for your true love. You've got a working vocabulary of flirty words, perfect phone call etiquette, and inviting body language. You have learned to give yourself guilt-free permission to have a social life, and your children will understand that when Mommy's world is happy, their world is a better place in which to live.

As you continue to put your 5 Finger Philosophy to the test, you will know in no uncertain terms when you meet the man with great REAL One potential. Then you can grow the care, concern, knowledge, respect, and connection that balance out to an unbreakable deep and fulfilling REALationship. Lacing your physical, mental, emotional, spiritual, and sexual fingers together with his is your ultimate goal of forever-after happiness. With a new man in your life or simply as a self-aware woman, explore and reawaken all the beautiful and sexy parts of you.

Whether you want to rescript your life as the traditional rock-and-paper design or simply stay in your defined heart space, it is your time to let go and trust that everything is happening perfectly at the right time in your life.

Visit me at <u>www.kerrizane.com</u>. *I'm there whenever you need me!*

You've gotten past all the stupid choices of your youth and you've had your beautiful kids. Now, just go and enjoy—have a good time!
—Mom.

 Kerri Zane is an Emmy award winning, twenty-year veteran television executive. A healthy living expert, single mom advisor, author, radio co-host and speaker. She has a master's degree in Spiritual Psychology from the University of Santa Monica, an undergraduate of UCLA, a member of NATAS, the Directors Guild of America, an ACE Certified Personal Trainer and Weight Management Consultant. The single mother of two daughters, for the last ten years, she lives in Long Beach, California.

Bibliography

Part One: The Inside 5

1. Rescript Your Life

Capacchione, L. (2000). *Visioning: Ten steps to designing the life of your dreams.* New York: Penguin Putnam.

Childhood trauma and adult mental health. (2011). Retrieved Oct. 5, 2011, from http://www.bps.org.uk/news/childhood-trauma-and-adult-mental-health.

Collier, R. (2008). The Secret of the Ages. Wilder Publications.

Dayton, T. (1994). Emotional sobriety: From relationship trauma to resilience and balance (pp. 8–11). Deerfield Beach, Florida: Health Communications, Inc.

Hulnick, H. R. & Hulnick, M. (2010). Loyalty to your soul. Carlsbad, California: Hay House.

Kalafut, M. Oxytocin: The cuddle and love hormone. Retrieved July 21, 2011 from http://molly.kalafut.org/misc/oxytocin.html.

Landmark Education http://www.landmarkeducation.com/

Loehr, J. and Schwartz, T. (2003) The Power of Full Engagement. New York, NY: The Free Press, A Division of Simon & Schuster, Inc.

University of Santa Monica Education http://www. universityofsantamonica.edu/

2. Fill Your Glass

Karasu, T. B. (2002). *The art of serenity: The path to a joyful life in the best and worst of times.* New York: Simon & Schuster.

Skolknick, A. (2002) Grounds for marriage: Reflections and research on an institution in transition. In M. Yalom, L. Carstensen, E. Freedman, & B. Gelpi, *Inside the American couple.* Berkeley, California: University of California Press Retrieved Oct. 22, 2011, from http://tinyurl.com/6bnbt4r.

New York University (2007, October 24). How The Brain Generates The Human Tendency For Optimism. Science Daily. Retrieved Nov. 34, 2011 from http://tinyurl.com/7knk2hv.

Oz, M., & Roizen, M. Happiness, generosity and positivity. Retrieved. Oct. 12, 2011, from http://www.youbeauty.com/mind/happiness-how-to-generous-positive.

Seligman, M. E. P. (2002). Authentic happiness: Using the new positive psychology to realize your potential for lasting fulfillment. New York: Free Press.

Seligman, M. E. P. (2006). Learned optimism: How to change your mind and your life. New York: Vintage Books.

Soussignan, R. (2002). Duchenne Smile, emotional experience, and automatic reactivity: A test of the facial feedback hypothesis. *Emotion, 2*(1), 52-74. DOI: 10.1037/1528-3542.2.1.52.

3. Flying in the Face of Fear

Jeffers, S. J. (1987). Feel the fear and do it anyway. New York: Ballantine Books.

4. Being "Me"

Fleet, C. B. & Harriet, S. Widows wear stilettos: A practical and emotional guide for the young widow. (2009). Far Hills, N.J.: New Horizon Press.

Giardina, R. Your authentic self. 2002. Hillsboro, Ore.: Beyond Words Publishing.

5. Right Here, Right Now

Campbell, S. (2001).Getting real. Novato, California: H. J. Kramer, Inc.

Dixit, J. (2008). The art of now: Six steps to living in the moment (Electronic version). Psychology Today. Retrieved March 12, 2011, from http://www.psychologytoday.com/articles/200810/the-art-now-six-steps-living-in-the-moment.

Langer, E. (1989). Mindfulness. Cambridge: Perseus Books.

Lyubomirsky, S. (2008).The How of Happiness. New York: Penguin Books.

Part Two: The Outside 5

6. Balance Your Multi-platforms

Brown, Nina. (2002). *Whose life is it anyway? When to stop taking care of their feelings and start taking care of your own.* Oakland, Calif.: New Harbinger Publications.

Hashe, Janis. Time management tips for single parents. Parenthood. com. August 2011 from http://www.parenthood.com/article-topics/time_management_tips_for_single_parents.html.

How to say no. August 2011 from http://www.wholeliving.com/article/how-to-say-no.

Little, Lori. (2005). Time Management for the successful single mom *Crosswalk.com*. August 2011 from http://www.crosswalk.com/parenting/1307606/.

Ury, Dr. William, PhD. (2007) "The power of a Positive no: How to say NO and still get to YES, New York, New York: Bantam Dell, A Division of Random House, Inc.

7. Retrofitting your financials

Bradford, S. (updated 2008). The five mistakes married women make. Retrieved Oct. 2, 2011, from http://tinyurl.com/bqqbxty.

Collaborative Divorce website materials. Retrieved Sept. 9, 2011, from http://www.collaborativedivorce.net/.

Georgaklis, H. (2011). 99 things women wish they knew before®... Planning for retirement. Clearwater, Florida: 99 Book Series, Inc.

Goudreau, J. (2010). Love and money: Step-by-step guide to financial unity. Retrieved Oct. 2, 2011, from http://tinyurl.com/c775o5c.

Rose, S. Divorce strategies for women. Retrieved Sept. 4, 2011, from http://www.DivorceStrategiesForWomen.com.

Stevenson, B. & Wolfers, J. (2007). Marriage Divorce: Changes and their Driving Forces. *Journal of Economic Perspectives, 21 (3),* 27–52. Retrieved Nov. 10, 2011 from http://bpp.wharton.upenn.edu/betseys/papers/JEP_Marriage_and_Divorce.pdf.

Todorova, A. (2008).The six financial mistakes couples make. Retrieved Oct. 2, 2011, from http://tinyurl.com/c88ospv.

Vacca Law website materials. Retrieved Sept. 9, 2011, from http://
www.vaccalaw.com/.

WomansDivorce.com website materials. Retrieved Oct. 4, 2011, from
http://www.womansdivorce.com/.

8. Love Your Vessel

American Society for Aesthetic Plastic Surgery. Cosmetic surgery
national data bank statistics for 1997 to 2007. Retrieved Sept.
25, 2011 from http://www.surgery.org/media/news-releases/117-
cosmetic-procedures-in-2007-.

Blumenthal, J. et al. (1999) Abstract: **Effects of exercise training
on older patients with major depression (Electronic Version).
1999.** *Archives of Internal Medicine.* **Retrieved Nov. 11, 2011,
from http://tinyurl.com/3hdn9ly.**

Build a better body image. Retrieved Nov. 11, 2011, from http://
tinyurl.com/7d86g9l.

Depression. (2011). Retrieved Sept. 14, 2011, from http://tinyurl.
com/ybebwmq.

Do attractive people get better treatment than others? (2001). Jet.

Eden, D. (2009). What makes us attractive? Viewzone. Retrieved Sept.
15, 2011 from http://www.viewzone.com/attractivenessx.html.

Frost, J. & McKelvie, S. J. (2005). The relationship of self-esteem
and body satisfaction to exercise activity for male and female
elementary school, high school, and university students. *Athletic
Insight.* Retrieved Sept. 3, 2011, from http://www.athleticinsight.
com/Vol7Iss4/Selfesteem.htm.

Goldberg, L. & Elliot, D. (2002). *The healing power of exercise: Your
guide to prevention and treating diabetes, depression, heart disease,
high blood pressure, arthritis, and more.* New York, New York: John
Wiley and Sons.

Gottlieb, L. (2010). *Marry him: The case for settling for Mr. Good Enough.* New York, New York: Dutton.

McAuley, E., Mihalko, S. L., & Bane, S. M. (1997). Exercise and self-esteem in middle-aged adults: Multidimensional relationships and physical fitness and self-efficacy influences. *Journal of Behavioral Medicine.* Retrieved Nov. 11, 2011, from http://tinyurl.com/85l2u77.

9. Put Your Game Face On

Diller, V. & Muir-Sukenick, J. (2010). Face it. Carlsbad, California: Hay House.

Lithwick, D. (2010) Our beauty bias is unfair. *Newsweek,* June 14. Retrieved Sept. 12, 2011, from http://tinyurl.com/7jmlwjx.

Meningaud, J.P., Benadiba, L., Servant, J.M., Herve, C., Bertrand, J.C., & Pelicier, Y. (2003). Depression, anxiety and quality of life: Outcome 9 months after facial cosmetic surgery. Depression, anxiety and quality of life: Outcome 9 months after facial cosmetic surgery. *Journal of Cranio-maxillofacial surgery,* Feb;31(1), 46–50.

Papadopulos N. A., Kovacs, L., Krammer, S., Herschbach, P., Henrich, G., & Biemer, E. (2007). Quality of life following aesthetic plastic surgery: A prospective study. *Journal of Plastic Reconstructive Aesthetic Surgery,* 60(8), 915–921.

Patzer, G. (2008). *Looks: Why they matter more than you ever imagined.* New York City, New York: AMACOM.

Reitzes, D. C. (2005). Self and health: Factors influencing self-esteem and functional health. Paper presented at the annual meeting of the American Sociological Association, Marriott Hotel, Loews Philadelphia Hotel, Philadelphia, PA Retrieved Sept. 1, 2011, from http://www.allacademic.com/meta/p18301_index.html.

Rhode, D. (2010). *The beauty bias: The injustice of appearance in life and law.* New York City, New York: Oxford University Press.

Ryall, J. (2009). Scientists unravel why women love makeup. *The Telegraph,* Jan. 21, 2009. Accessed Oct. 2, 2011, from http://tinyurl.com/6r7my9g.

Sadick, N. (2008). The impact of cosmetic interventions on quality of life. *Dermatology Online Journal, 14(8).* Retrieved Oct. 14, 2011, from http://dermatology.cdlib.org/148/commentary/qualityoflife/sadick.html.

Sommer, B, Zschocke, I, Bergfeld, D, Sattler. G, & Augustin M. (2003). Satisfaction of patients after treatment with botulinum toxin for dynamic facial lines, Dermatologic Surgery, 29:456-460. Abstract retrieved Nov. 24, 2011 from http://www.ncbi.nlm.nih.gov/pubmed/12752511.

Teal, A. Three ways that low self-esteem can affect a relationship. (2009). Retrieved Oct. 2, 2011, from http://tinyurl.com/7l8ukga.

Well-being: Skin deeper and deeper. Retrieved Oct. 18, 2011, from http://tinyurl.com/cpkjb6b.

10. Sex and Sexability

http://www.amjmed.com/article/PIIS0002934311006553/fulltext January 2012.

Block, Joel D. (2008) Sex over 50. New York City, New York: Perigee Books.

Burnett, M. & McAnulty, R. (2006). *Sex and sexuality, volume 1.* Westport, Connecticut: Praeger Publishers.

Cohen, R. (2011). Maintaining healthy levels of testosterone. Retrieved Sept. 5 from http://www.thehormoneshop.com/maintainingtestosterone.htm.

Deida, D. (2005). *Dear lover: A woman's guide to enjoying love's deepest bliss.* Boulder, Colorado: Sounds True, Inc.

Janssen, E, Heiman, J., Sanders, S., Hahn, S., Holtzworth, A., Fortenberry, D. et al. Marriage and sexual health. Research abstract, retrieved Sept. 5, 2011 from http://www.kinseyinstitute. org/research/marriage_health.html

Dr. James Houran a study for online dating magazine. http://www. onlinedatingmagazine.com/about/drjimhouran.html

Kao, A., PhD, Binik, Y., Kapuscinski, A., & Khalifé, S. (2008). Dyspareunia in postmenopausal women: A critical review. Pain research & management, 13(3): 243–254. Accessed Nov. 12, 2011, from http://www.ncbi.nlm.nih.gov/pmc/articles/ PMC2671314/.

Kearney-Cooke, A. (2004). Change your mind, change your body: Feeling good about your body and self after 40. New York City, New York: Atria Books.

Kinsey, A. (1998). *Sexual behavior in the human male.* Bloomington, Indiana: Indiana University Press.

Lynn, D. & Spitzer, C. (2010). *Sex for grownups: Dr. Dorree reveals the truths, lies and must-tries for great sex after 50.* Deerfield Beach, Florida: Healthy Communications, Inc.

Menopause. Retrieved Nov. 14, 2011, from http://www.nlm.nih.gov/ medlineplus/menopause.html.

Schroeder, J. (2007). Exercise and menopause: A research review. IDEA Health and Fitness Conference Workshop. Accessed Sept. 24 from http://www.ideafit.com/conference/idea-world-fitness-convention-2007/exercise-and-menopause-a-research-review.

Stewart, D. E. (2005). Menopause: A mental health practitioner's guide. Arlington, Virginia: American Psychiatric Publishing.

Schiff, I. (2000–2002) The benefits of regular exercise. Retrieved Sept. 10 from http://www.holisticonline.com/remedies/hrt/hrt_exercise. htm.

Part Three: The "Real One" 5

11. Be a Flirty Girl

Collingwood, J. (2006). Modern love: Ways women can be more assertive. *Psych Central.* Retrieved on December 5, 2011, from http://psychcentral.com/lib/2006/modern-love-ways-women-can-be-more-assertive/.

Damasio, A. (2010). Self comes to mind: Constructing the conscious brain. New York City, New York: Pantheon Books.

Dunn, Susan. *Midlife dating survival manual for women.* Available in eBook format from http://www.susandunn.cc/midlife_dating_manual.html.

Moore, M. M. (1985). Nonverbal courtship patterns in women: Context and consequences. *Ethology and Sociobiology, 64,* 237-247.

Northrup, C. (2011).Flirting online and infidelity: Is this our new norm? *Huffington Post.* Retrieved Oct. 14 from http://www.huffingtonpost.com/chrisanna-northrup/flirting-online-and-infid_b_880896.html.

Social Issues Research Center. (2004). The Flirting Report. Retrieved Oct. 14, 2011 from http://www.sirc.org/publik/flirt2.pdf.

12. Diving into the Dating Pool

Fisher, E.S. (2005). Mom, there is a man in your kitchen and he's wearing your robe. Cambridge, Massachusetts: Da Capo Press.

Frances, L. (2006). *Dating mating and manhandling: An ornithologist's guide to men.* New York City, New York: Harmony Books.

McKenna, S. (2006). *Sex and the single mom.* Berkeley, California: Ten Speed Press.

Sills, J. (2009). *Getting naked again.* New York City, New York: Springboard Press.

Sbrochi, M. (2010). *Stop looking for a husband: Find the love of your life.* Dallas, Texas: Brown Books Publishing.

13. Enjoy the Journey

Carpenter, L. M., Nathanson, C. A., & Young J. K. 2006. "Sex After 40?: Gender, Ageism, and Sexual Partnering in Midlife." Journal of Aging Studies 20(2): 93-106.

Current online dating and dating services facts & statistics. (1992–2011). Retrieved Dec. 2, 2011 from http://www.datingsitesreviews.com/staticpages/index.php?page=online.

Gottlieb, L. (2010). *Marry him: The case for settling for Mr. Good Enough.* New York, New York: Dutton.

Kantrowitz, B. (2009, June). "Counter-cougar thinking." Message posted to http://www.thedailybeast.com/newsweek/2009/05/28/counter-cougar-thinking.html

Romm, S. (2005). Dating after 50: Negotiating the minefields of midlife romance. Fresno, California: Quill Driver Books.

14. The 5 Finger Philosophy

Ferrucci, P. (2004). What we may be: techniques for psychological and spiritual growth through psychosynthesis. New York: Most Tarcher/Penguin Books.

Ruiz, D. M. (1997). The Four Agreements. San Rafael, California: Amber-Allen Publishing, Inc.

15. Rock, Paper, Hearts

Babcock, D.E. Marriage was made for people—people were not made for marriage. Retrieved Oct. 11, 2011, from http://www.selfgrowth.com/articles/Marriage_Was_Made_For_People_-_People_Were_Not_Made_For_Marriage.html.

Corso, R. & Staff. (2010). Annual happiness index find one third of Americans are very happy. Retrieved Oct. 11, 2011, from http://tinyurl.com/85fop2p.

Fisher, H. (2004). Why We Love: The Nature and Chemistry of Romantic Love. New York City, New York: Henry Holt and Company.

Friedman, H.S., & Martin, L. (2011). The myths of living longer. *Parade* magazine. Retrieved Oct. 12, 2012, from http://www.parade.com/health/2011/02/20-the-myths-of-living-longer.html.

King, L.W. (translator). (2008). The Code of Hammurabi. Retrieved Dec. 19, 2011, at http://avalon.law.yale.edu/ancient/hamframe.asp.

Levine, S.B. (2005). *Inventing the rest of our lives.* New York City, New York: Viking Penguin.

Osho. (2007). *Emotional wellness: Transforming fear, anger, and jealousy into creative energy.* New York City, New York: Harmony Books.

Osho. (2008). *Being in love: How to love with awareness and relate without fear.* New York City, New York: Harmony Books.

Pew Social Trends Staff. (2010). The decline of marriage and rise of new families. Retrieved Oct. 9, 2011 from http://www.pewsocialtrends.org/2010/11/18/the-decline-of-marriage-and-rise-of-new-families/.

Richo, D. (2000). *How to be an adult in relationships.* Boston, Massachusetts: Shambhala Books.

Ruiz, D. M. (1999). *The Mastery of Love*. San Rafael, California: Amber-Allen Publishing, Inc.

63 interesting facts about marriage. (2009). Retrieved Nov. 10, 2011 from *http://facts.randomhistory.com/interesting-facts-about-marriage. html.*

Stony Brook University. (2010). Love can last: SBU imaging study shows brain activity of those in love long term similar to those newly in love. Press release retrieved Nov. 2, 2011 from http:// tinyurl.com/646s54b.

The Lewis Terman Study at Stanford University. Abstract retrieved Dec. 2, 2011, from http://www.cpc.unc.edu/projects/lifecourse/ research_projects/terman.

Tzadok, A.B. (1997). The concept of soulmates in Torah & Kabbalah. Retrieved Oct. 23, 2011, from http://www.hashkafah.com/index. php?/topic/64131-the-concept-of-soulmates/.

Worldwide divorce statistics. (2011). Retrieved Oct. 11, 2011 from http://www.divorce.com/article/worldwide-divorce-statistics.

CPSIA information can be obtained at www.ICGtesting.com
Printed in the USA
LVOW07s1114281014

410866LV00002B/156/P